Wooden Spoon Society

RUGBY WORLD '01

EDITED BY

Ian Robertson

Queen Anne Press

A QUEEN ANNE PRESS BOOK

© Lennard Associates Limited 2000

First published in 2000 by
Queen Anne Press, a division of
Lennard Associates Limited
Mackerye End
Harpenden, Herts AL5 5DR

A catalogue entry is available from the British Library

ISBN 1 85291 629 X (paperback)
ISBN 1 85291 628 1 (hardback)

Production Editor: Chris Marshall
Cover Design/Design Consultant: Paul Cooper
Reproduction: Colour Image
Printed and bound in Slovenia

The publishers would like to thank Colorsport and SpedeGrafix 99 for
providing most of the photographs for this book.

The publishers would also like to thank AllsportUK, David Gibson
(Fotosport), Hill & Knowlton, Inphopics, Peter Jordan, Sponsorship
Bureau, Terry Sellick, Slattery PR and Chris Thau for additional
material.

CONTENTS

We're proud to support the
Wooden Spoon Society.

 Lloyds TSB
Your life. Your bank

FOREWORD

BY HRH THE PRINCESS ROYAL

BUCKINGHAM PALACE

It again gives me great pleasure to write the foreword to this book which continues to reflect the involvement of the Wooden Spoon Society with the game of rugby.

As Patron of the Society, I am pleased to note that it continues to grow and develop. This is reflected in some excellent community projects completed in the past year:-

I was able to open the Wooden Spoon Society Building for the ACE (Aiding Communication in Education) Centre Advisory Trust in Oxford giving wonderful support in the complex needs of physically disabled children with communication difficulties.

The three previous World Cup Captains opened Wooden Spoon House in Blackwood in South Wales as a Resource Centre and Respite Home for disabled children in that community.

Later this year I will open the Wooden Spoon Child Development Centre in Lambeth which will focus attention on children with problems of multiple disabilities and high risk diseases.

In the game of rugby Wooden Spoon has assisted with bringing the game to inner city areas of Newcastle, Dudley and London and has also supported the work of the Welsh Rugby Union Charitable Trust.

BUCKINGHAM PALACE

It gives me great pleasure to see that the acceptance of the Wooden Spoon Society as the charity of British Rugby grows apace and this book is again a reflection of that.

Enjoy the book and support the charity which does so much for children and young people through the great game of rugby football.

Wooden Spoon Society
- the Charity of British Rugby

Royal Patron: HRH The Princess Royal
Patrons: Rugby Football Union • Scottish Rugby Union
                Welsh Rugby Union • Irish Rugby Football Union

'It's not what we do... it's what we do with the money!'

WRU Chairman Glanmor Griffiths gets the cash from Welsh Spoon President Bob Norster to fund the Wooden Spoon Wheelchair Terraces at the Millennium Stadium, Cardiff.

Wooden Spoon Society has a well-deserved reputation for putting on a 'first-class do'! Hundreds of thousands of pounds pour into the Spoon coffers every year from our high-profile events. Rugby dinners, golf days, cash from our network of 22 Regional Committees covering the United Kingdom, and certainly not least the 'mountains of monies' that are generated each year from our Spoon Challenges, the Vauxhall Four Peaks Challenge and the Ford Great Lakeland Challenge. This year the Wooden Spoon Society Four Peaks Challenge dwarfed them all with a massive £471,732.20 in pledges! As we always recover in excess of our pledged amounts, there is even more to come! However, it's what we *do* with the money that counts. We thought a little reflection on this would not come amiss in this Millennium Edition of our annual.

We have now spent consistently over a million pounds each year for the past three years and, over the next 27 months, a further £4.3 million pounds worth of projects will emerge suitably badged Wooden Spoon Society. Some of these projects have been quite magical in their development, quite wondrous in their benefit to the children and young people who have enjoyed their umbrella of comfort and warmth. We only undertake capital projects that we can badge; that way our members can have a rewarding glow of recognition when they reflect upon how effective their fund-raising has been.

In 1995 Diana Princess of Wales opened the Wooden Spoon Society Pre-School Centre in Solihull (£580,000) for children who because of age are outside the education system and who are physically, mentally and socially disadvantaged – a haven for parents desperate for guidance-counselling and sound medical advice. Later, in 1996 we launched and completed our Wooden Spoon Society Lineham Farm Project, just outside Leeds (£300,000); this is a farm that now gives over 1,200 holidays each year to the disadvantaged children of the city and its environs.

A couple of years after that, we opened the first Wooden Spoon Society Teenage Cancer Trust Unit at the Christie Hospital, Manchester (£560,000), and followed on with

another Wooden Spoon Society Teenage Cancer Trust Unit at Queen Elizabeth Hospital, Birmingham (£486,000), which was opened this year. These two units are dedicated to teenagers, who are treated within their own peer group and now have, statistics suggest, a 15 per cent increased chance of beating this terrible enemy.

Above: The ACE Centre at Oxford, housed in the Wooden Spoon Building.

To Meadow Wood School, Pinner, North London, we gave a highly effective Wooden Spoon Society Hydrotherapy Pool (£340,000), which is the envy of all. Talking of pools, in Macclesfield, at Lambs House School for Autistic Children, we provided a superb swimming facility (£66,000) with aid from our great corporate friends TNT UK Limited. Water is a balm that soothes and massages the most unresponsive mind and muscle.

Our Royal Patron, The Princess Royal, loved her visit to the Wooden Spoon Society ACE Centre in Oxford (£700,000), a fantastic set-up for helping children with severe learning difficulties. ACE stands for Aiding Communication in Education and assesses children with physical disabilities such as cerebral palsy to see what modern technology can do to assist communication and some physical aptitudes. In the year 2000 two further major projects will be opened. The Wooden Spoon Society Family Cancer Care and Haematology Unit at Stoke Mandeville Hospital (£900,000) and, in the London Borough of Lambeth, the first Child Development Centre. This initiative, under the auspices of the government's Health Action Zone for Children, will be housed in Wooden Spoon House, Lambeth, at a total cost in excess of £2.3 million.

Below: HRH The Princess Royal opens another Wooden Spoon Project, this time for Sense Scotland.

These are just some of the major National Projects that we have undertaken, but perhaps even more important is the plethora of Regional Projects. Our philosophy of Local Funds for Local Projects allows each of our regions to keep every penny they raise, and we, from a central fund, then double that money on a pound-for-pound basis. This allows us to consider ourselves a local charity with a national emphasis, but the important thing is that *where the money is raised is where it is spent*. Each of our Regional Committees makes a contribution to *their* community with *their* money, but we make it worth double!

None of this would have been possible were it not for the compassion of many players, spectators, officials and media representatives of the game of rugby. Their support, both vocal and practical, good humour and bounteous pockets help with the work of Wooden Spoon Society. It is greatly rewarding to reflect that we enjoy a niche within rugby which provides a perennial source of goodwill and generosity. Rugby is in our heart and rugby is the badge on our kit. The community is where we live and operate and it is to the benefit of the community that the game of rugby has proved itself such a wonderful social leveller, opportunity enhancer and enjoyment provider.

In the modern era rugby has undergone some fairly dramatic changes that may in the future affect the basic culture of the game. However, its heart remains strong, it beats in overall pursuit of happiness and wellbeing, and hopefully the Wooden Spoon Society will continue to reflect its aspirations, its enjoyment, its compassion and its commitment to offering children and young people a better life and a better opportunity.

Above: Our 'Enery unveils the Wooden Spoon Society Wing at the Ridge School, Tonbridge.
Left: John Inverdale opens the Wooden Spoon Cabin for the Surrey Committee.
Below: The Three Captains (Kirk, Farr-Jones and Pienaar) open the Wooden Spoon Society Respite Care Home in Blackwood, Wales.

Why not join us in making the Spoon even bigger and better? What other charity appeals so effectively to lovers of rugby and all sports, can make local folks feel proudly part of a national organisation and, best of all, doubles your money?! Details of membership of Spoon can be had from:

The Spoon Office,
35 Maugham Court,
Whitstable, Kent CT5 4RR
Tel: 01227 772295
e-mail:
charity@woodenspoonsoc.org.uk
website:
www.woodenspoonsoc.org.uk

'I often show visitors round Meadow Wood, and am always proud to show off both our building and the work that goes on in it. But if I time it right, and I show the pool in use – what an impact! First, the pool itself is warm, bright and very inviting. Then, in the water are children who have severe disablilities enjoying themselves hugely. Most of the children move much better in the water than they do out of it, and some are able to move independently… But it isn't just 'swimming', it is physiotherapy, and also a great deal of the school's curriculum is taught in this setting. So thanks again to the Wooden Spoon Society for helping us to create such a wonderful asset for our pupils.'
John Addison,
Headmaster,
Meadow Wood School

Left and bottom of previous page: The Wooden Spoon Society Family Cancer Unit at Stoke Mandeville rises out of the ground.

Left: Lineham Farm, a magic place for children.
Below: An artist's impression of the Millennium Project – the Wooden Spoon Society Child Development Centre in Lambeth, London.

SUPPORTING TOWN HOUSES, COUNTRY HOUSES & BRICK HOUSES.

Cheltenham & Gloucester

www.cheltglos.co.uk

Cheltenham & Gloucester plc   Registered in England No. 2299428
Registered Office Barnett Way Gloucester GL4 3RL

COMMENT

QUIS CUSTODIET IPSOS CUSTODES?

BY **PAUL STEPHENS**

Clive Woodward's England might have had the summer to themselves. From a purely British point of view – David Coulthard's Formula One victories at Monaco and Magny-Cours being the exception – there appeared to be no end to the dreadful sporting news in June and July: Kevin Keegan's footballers bombed out of Euro 2000, Nasser Hussain's cricketers were roundly defeated in the Edgbaston Test, Tim Henman's expectations of becoming the first Briton to win the men's singles at Wimbledon for 64 years were blasted to destruction by Mark Philippoussis, and Britain's Davis Cup hopes were torpedoed by Ecuador.

Woodward's luck held as Martin Johnson's team stayed in the spotlight until the unforgettable Lord's Test, by which time England had returned from the Rainbow Nation unlucky perhaps to have merely drawn the series with the Springboks rather than won it. Even though it is so devilishly difficult to win in South Africa, Nick Mallett's charges were then a team in transition, as was confirmed in their thumping defeat by Australia a couple of weeks later. Not that Woodward should rue his luck, for he was fortunate to still be in charge of England after their previous meeting with South Africa, when they were bundled so ingloriously out of the World Cup in Paris.

Clive Woodward need not have worried. Despite asking to be judged on his team's performances in the World Cup, the England coach was awarded a new contract by the Rugby Football Union.

Ian McGeechan's meticulous preparation denied England a Grand Slam at Murrayfield.

Having asked to be judged on his performance in the global competition, Woodward could have harboured few complaints if his contract had been terminated soon after England's quarter-final defeat. For the big prizes continue to elude Woodward, through whose grasp two Grand Slams have also slipped, as he has stumbled to come to terms with the tactical and technical necessities at the highest level, despite having resources which are the envy of the rugby-playing world.

How else can we explain how England allowed Scotland to sucker them to defeat in the Calcutta Cup match at Murrayfield, in which England attempted to play dry-weather rugby on a day which was graced by storms of which the good folk of Invercargill would have been proud. The forecasts for heavy rain and sleet had been evident on the Monday before the match and worsened as the week went on. It was a foresight saga England could draw no pleasure from having played a part in.

Notwithstanding that the weather forebodings were ignored, Woodward waited for the Scotland coach, Ian McGeechan, to prove the point that Garath Archer is temperamentally unsuited to international rugby. Once the Scotland second-rowers, Scott Murray and Richard Metcalfe, got up Archer's nose, the England line out became a shambles. That could have been put right if Woodward could have called Martin Johnson off the bench. But Johnson – the best lock forward in the world and fresh, having played only four games after returning from long-term injury – was not among Woodward's replacements. England subsided to ignominious defeat as Scotland exposed one folly after another. In the process a second successive Grand Slam had been cast to the wind.

If the senior England team had been unmasked once again for their inability to think on their feet and introduce some variety to their game plan, England A added plenty of variety to their team, without ever coming near to producing a convincing game plan. There is now plenty to play for at this level, with a recognisable Six Nations Championship for A teams. The media, slow to welcome the new competition, eventually acknowledged it as worthwhile by printing the table throughout the

Martin Johnson takes on the might of Fiji in the World Cup. The world's best lock forward was not even on the bench for the Calcutta Cup match.

tournament, which is a step forward from the previous year when Wales were unheralded Grand Slam winners of the second tier.

England's response was to raise the temperature above lukewarm only once, in their final match, against Scotland at Goldenacre, by which time it was too late, and they deserved to finish no higher than fourth in the table, above the Scots and Italy. Along the way, coach Richard Hill made changes with all the alacrity of a Japanese car maker to a model range. After the defeat by Ireland at Northampton, Hill made ten changes for the match against France. Five more followed against Wales, another nine for the Italy game, and a further five to face Scotland. For each game Hill chose a different captain, and across the five matches he used six centres, three scrum halves and seven lock forwards. Without the continuity of selection so essential to team-building, and with no clear sense of purpose or direction, it is no wonder England A wallowed. Mind you, Woodward was nowhere to be seen at any of the matches, so at least he wasn't required to watch the A team's erratic progress in what should be the most important of all proving grounds for testing and developing England's most talented uncapped players.

It would be unreasonable to expect Woodward to shoulder all the blame for this unhealthy situation, any more than for the poor showing of the England U21 team, who struggled in Europe before falling dismally short of expectations in the summer's SANZAR tournament. But someone has to take responsibility for the nation's underperforming representative teams, and it should be a matter of serious concern that the wealthiest of all the European nations is unable to do better. For starters, regular

A-team tours to the southern hemisphere would not only be helpful in developing our most promising players but could bring benefits to those who aspire to coach at the highest level; especially as there are so many overseas coaches in the English club game.

It is of little comfort to know that, in spite of these disappointments, money and good quality players are not a problem for Woodward, supported as he is by a Board of Management at the Rugby Football Union who have become as tolerant of failure as they have been inept in their dealings with the clubs in the Allied Dunbar Premiership. It is as well for Woodward that he possesses a similar sort of easy, boyish charm to John Major – along with a fairly thick skin – although just as they did for the former prime minister, serious doubts remain over his fitness for the number one job.

After Holland were beaten by Italy on penalties in their Euro 2000 semi-final, their coach, Frank Rijkaard, resigned. Within hours of the last whistle in the final, Italy's coach, Dino Zoff, decided it was time for him to go after his team had been beaten by France. But the resignation route was never an option for Woodward, who chose instead to open negotiations on a fresh contract before his first expired in August, so that a new one would be in place in advance of the squad's departure for South Africa. Perhaps because Woodward is a genuinely nice man and continuity is so much more agreeable than change, or maybe because there were so few alternatives, the RFU agreed to Woodward's demands and signed him up until the next World Cup.

If the RFU's myopic refusal to acknowledge Woodward's shortcomings sounds depressingly familiar, then their part in negotiations with the Premiership clubs and a transparent lack of direction and sure handling in so many other areas of the game amount to nothing short of a scandal. With few of the Premiership clubs able to find agreement on the major issues, the RFU appears divided on the way ahead. Consequently, there are no obvious signs of the leadership so vital if the club game is to prosper or give the impression of having anything more than the faintest idea of where it wants to go.

Worcester's chief executive, Geoff Cooke: 'Promotion and relegation between the divisions must be sacrosanct.'

Wherever they go, the Premiership One clubs have no intention of taking any of their brethren from Premiership Two with them. In a breathtakingly arrogant display of self-interest the top stratum got its way over the issue of automatic promotion and relegation last season, when there was a play-off between the bottom club in One and the top club in Two. Once the content of the Rob Andrew Plan was revealed, it was clear that if the plan was adopted ADP One would be ring-fenced for a number of seasons, leaving those in ADP Two with nowhere to go but down. The RFU raised not a murmur of dissent at this blatant act of protectionism, which is a denial of the essential fairness in a league system with promotion and relegation. Geoff Cooke, the former England manager and now chief executive of Division Two Worcester, was incensed by the proposal: 'Some of the clubs in Division One, like Newcastle, Northampton, Bristol and Saracens, have forgotten where they have come from. All of them have spent

Worrying times for Saracens' owner, Nigel Wray, who has seen attendances at Vicarage Road plummet by over 22 per cent in two seasons.

some time in Division Two, and would still be there were it not for the principle of promotion. In my view, promotion and relegation should be sacrosant.'

Were this the only problem faced by the RFU and the clubs, those who care for the game could feel reasonably content that the transition to professionalism had been in capable hands. But just as the numbers increase daily of those unsure of the Blair government's ability to manage the affairs of state, so there is increasing evidence of a growing lack of confidence in the RFU's unconvincing management and woeful leadership. However, the clubs themselves can hardly expect to avoid censure, given their calamitous housekeeping and the appalling state of their collective finances.

Not until late July, when the Allied Dunbar Premiership was renamed the Zurich Premiership, were the clubs able to agree upon a fixture list for the new season, which by then was a mere five weeks away. Nor for that matter could they find one voice in the acceptance of a British Cup, to replace the Tetley's Bitter Cup. The sponsor's response to this dismal piece of commercial prevarication doesn't bear recall. But had Tetley's judgment been such that there was no future for them in the union game, then the RFU would be waving goodbye to them, just as they have to Jewson, and the other brewers, Thwaites, who until last season sponsored the Northern Leagues.

Against this uncertain background, the clubs announced gleefully that the paying public were flocking to the game in ever-increasing numbers. Moreover, as ticket-discounting was in decline, the figures were more robust than for earlier seasons. It sounded like a fine piece of spin, which, on closer examination, proved to be so. In the 1998-99 season, the average Division One gate was 5,507. Last season this increased to 5,702. On the face of it an improvement of 3.6 per cent. Although what English Rugby Partnership – who represent the interests of the Premiership clubs – didn't say was that the average in 1997-98 was 6,478. In other words there has been a shortfall in two seasons of 12 per cent. If that fact does not send out clear signals to those who expect us to believe the hokum about how wonderful things are for the clubs in England, then close examination of the Saracens figures surely will.

The average Premiership attendances at Vicarage Road have nosedived from a high of 9,303 in 1997-98 to 7,250 last season; a fall of over 22 per cent. At Wasps there has been a two-year slump of 15.7 per cent. Only at Northampton and Gloucester have there been any worthwhile gains, while even Bath and champions Leicester have been obliged to address a shortfall. No wonder the clubs want more money from the RFU to help finance the overblown playing contracts, to recruit more overseas players, and so redress the decline in gate monies.

Most disheartening of all is the realisation that the clubs and the RFU have been given an easy ride by the media, who have either swallowed the hype or, as some newspaper sports editors have decreed, stopped concentrating on what happens off the field, because the readers have had enough of the incessant wrangling and grotesque politics.

The RFU are the guardians of our game. It is time for them to abandon the Wilsonian approach that has bedevilled the way in which they have faced the difficulties which beset rugby. It will no longer suffice to believe, as Harold Wilson was prone to do, that if one ignores a problem for long enough it will eventually go away.

London Irish are to play at their third home in as many seasons and will do well to half-fill the Madejski Stadium.

Juvenal in his *Satires* posed the vexing question for situations in which we have little confidence in those appointed to positions of trust, when he asked: '*Quis custodiet ipsos custodes*?' Who will guard the guards themselves? It is a question we need to ask ourselves again. And Again. And Again.

NEXT

Official Clothing Sponsors Leicester Tigers

A QUESTION OF ELIGIBILITY

BY **NICK CAIN**

To be, or not to be, in terms of eligibility? The Bard may not have intended it quite like that, but that was the question that had Welsh, Scottish and IRB rugby administrators in a spin for the best part of March and April. Eligibility became an unwelcome spectre at the Six Nations feast, as the rights of Shane Howarth and Brett Sinkinson, the two Welsh Kiwis, and David Hilton, Scotland's Bristol born-and-bred butcher, to play for their adopted countries were filleted with precision by the British press, forcing the International Rugby Board (IRB) to enforce its own regulations with at least a semblance of rigour.

The result was not one that the game, and in particular its administrators at international level, could take any pride in. Not least, it brought the curtain down on the representative career of Howarth. Sinkinson and Hilton can requalify through residency, although time is not on their side. The culpability that can be laid at the doors of Howarth, Sinkinson and Hilton, all of whom were popular men within their adopted squads, lay in a desire to play international rugby which overrode the zealousness with which they checked their family histories. But although this left them open to accusations of being more than a little economical with the truth, the players would never have been in the dock if the IRB and its constituent national unions – in this instance Wales and Scotland – had not made such a botch of policing their own regulations.

Above: Brett Sinkinson
on the charge for Wales
against Japan in RWC
1999. The 29-year-old
flanker will now have to
qualify by residency
before he can play for
Wales again.
Previous page: Shane
Howarth was stymied
by the IRB nationality
laws introduced on 1
January. He cannot now
qualify for Wales by
residency because he
played for New Zealand.
Howarth, a full back
who galvanised Wales
with his attacking verve,
is here in action against
Samoa in RWC 1999.

Under IRB regulations a player can play only for a country in which he was born, or in which a parent or one grandparent was born. The only other means of qualifying is for the player to complete three years of consecutive residence in his adopted country. However, after records in New Zealand were searched, the Welsh Rugby Union (WRU) were left with faces as red as their jerseys when Howarth's claim to be 'a walking Grand Slam', with eligibility for Wales through a Cardiff-born grandfather, could not be substantiated. The same search showed that Sinkinson's grandfather, Sydney, was born in Oldham, Lancashire, and not Carmarthen, as had been claimed. And if his agent's subsequent claim that 'It didn't matter because Oldham is near Wales' was not farcical enough, there was more to come. No sooner had the bogus Welsh qualifications been revealed than the Scottish Rugby Union (SRU) admitted that it had not requested birth certificate evidence that Hilton's grandfather, Walter, had been born in Edinburgh. When the said certificate was produced it duly revealed that Walter had been born in Bristol.

The story behind how the matter first came to light through the revelations about Sinkinson and Howarth provides an insight into the often Byzantine world of international rugby. There had been endless rumours about Sinkinson, but most of them were considered to be puffs of hot air until Richard Bath, the sports editor of the *Sunday Herald* in Glasgow, followed one of them up with a view to finding out more about the eligibility of not only Sinkinson but also Scotland's growing band of 'Kilted Kiwis'. In a casual conversation with an agent in Australia, the agent suggested to Bath that Murrayfield was not particularly strict on calling for proof of eligibility. He added that he had had New Zealand players trying to pass themselves off as Scots.

Bath discovered that trying to check birth certificates in the UK was hugely time-consuming, and he contacted Joseph Romanos, a New Zealand journalist. Romanos lived in Upper Hutt, which, conveniently, is where the New Zealand Births & Deaths Office is located. The way their birth certificates are structured makes checking back easier than it is in the UK, so Bath paid him to check the antecedents of the Scottish Kiwis, Sinkinson and Howarth. Bath had expected that Sinkinson's credentials might not stack up, but the absence of Howarth's Cardiff-born grandad caught him and the rest of the rugby world by complete surprise. A week later the Hilton story surfaced, as did the revelation that Scotland had given 24 caps to Peter Walton, another Englishman, despite the fact that he failed to qualify on either a residential or grandparental basis. It also emerged that Tyrone Maullin, a South African lock with Swansea who had played for Wales in a non-cap match against America, and Jon Stuart, a former Leicester centre who had been selected for Scotland A, were both ineligible until they had served the residency qualification.

The low point in the sorry saga came when the SRU decided that, as far as they were concerned, Hilton remained eligible for selection. Bill Watson,

Above: Back-row forward Peter Walton gained 24 Scotland caps without being qualified on either a residential or grandparental basis.
Left: Like Brett Sinkinson, David Hilton (right), seen here with Paul Burnell and Robert Russell, has a chance to resurrect his international career once his residential qualification period is up – in August 2002, if he remains in Scotland.

the SRU's chief executive, provided this explanation: 'His family have signed an affidavit confirming that all understood David's grandfather was born in Edinburgh. David was a product of the Scottish Exiles system and first won selection when eligibility was taken on trust.' That was too much even for the IRB, and the SRU were instructed that Hilton would be unavailable until the enquiry was over.

No less bizarre was Howarth's search for the elusive Tom Williams, his Welsh grandfather. The plot thickened when it was suggested that the reason Tom's name was omitted from the Howarth family tree was because he had had an affair with Shane's Maori grandmother, Hene Maaka. However, the trail went cold when she denied that she had an affair with the mysterious Welshman.

Yet, despite all the twists as the players sought to cling onto their international careers, the blame attached to the WRU and the SRU deserved to be far greater than that attached to the players. The desire of coaches to strengthen their squads should at no stage have been allowed to persuade the unions to transgress IRB regulations either in letter or spirit by failing to do the proper checks on birth certificates. If in doubt, the unions should have referred eligibility cases to the IRB. The only mitigating factor in favour of the WRU or the SRU is that, although theirs are the most flagrant breaches of eligibility law in recent seasons, there is not a single one of the big eight rugby nations which has not been culpable of bending the rules in their own favour at one time or other in the post-war international era. It is not much of a defence.

The biggest disappointment in the eligibility fiasco was the way the IRB tried to absolve itself of any responsibility for the root causes. In the process it appeared like a limp, buck-passing parody of a world governing body. Not only did the IRB fail to acknowledge the abject failure of its flawed decision to expect those with a vested interest in the outcome, the national unions, to police against their own interests, we also had sermons from Stephen Baines, the IRB's chief executive, on an almost daily basis, stressing how gravely he viewed the breaches. The only problem was that he said precisely nothing about how the problem should be tackled.

This did little to convince anyone that the IRB's eventual appointment of a three-man judicial committee would come up with anything new, as most of the serious detective work had already been done for them by the press. It duly declared the three players ineligible and banned them from playing international rugby until they qualified through residency. Howarth, 31, was the main casualty. Because he had already been capped by New Zealand, the new IRB nationality laws introduced on 1 January, which prohibit a player from representing more than one country irrespective of residency, ruled Howarth out where they hadn't when Wales claimed him in November 1998. Sinkinson, 29, has 14 months to wait before Wales can consider picking him again at open-side, and Hilton, 30, will requalify if he stays in Scotland until August 2002, when he will be 32.

The IRB also, belatedly, took some responsibility for checking birth certificates of those claiming international transfer rights through grandparents and parents, although not without a degree of ambiguity. 'We are compiling a database of every eligible union,' said Baines. 'The responsibility to check documentation still rests with individual unions. That used to be taken on trust. That is no longer good enough.' Although Baines defended the IRB for not having vetted eligibility claims in the past on the basis that the logistics would have been too difficult, it is hard to understand what is so logistically demanding about each union having to submit either a birth certificate or a residency certificate before an adopted player is cleared. Nor is it easy to see how the policing would be difficult. No certificate, no player, sounds simple enough.

That the administrators were content to let the players carry the can was also evident in the IRB's leniency towards the WRU and the SRU. The judicial commission, chaired by Jannie Lubbe (South Africa) and including Ronnie Dawson (Ireland) and John Spencer (England), decided that it was outside its brief to take action against officials and left it up to the WRU and SRU to decide whether they would take action against specific officials or players of their own. Some chance. The only punishment for the unions was having to pay the costs for the IRB's two-day hearing in Dublin.

There is no doubt that the eligibility revelations made rugby a laughing stock. The Australian Rugby Union (ARU), which in recent times has been conspicuously self-important, lambasted the Welsh and Scots for failing to comply with the IRB regulations. The only problem was that the ARU, having cherry-picked a few notable players from other countries itself, was in no position to lecture. Nor did its suggestion that grandparental qualifications should be dispensed with find favour with the other member unions of the IRB. At least rugby's international governing body got that right. Hopefully, the IRB will now realise that it's not so much where you draw the line in the sand that matters – and grandparents and three-year residency are appropriate markers – but how determined you are to make sure it is not crossed.

Jon Stuart playing for Leicester against Wasps in November 1998. Stuart was chosen for Scotland A but was in fact ineligible until he had satisfied the residency requirement.

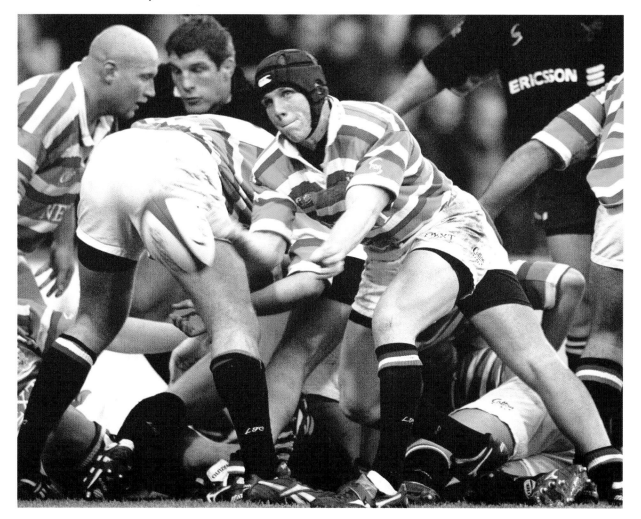

RUGBY WORLDWIDE

NEW SOUTHERN STARS

BY **RAECHELLE EDWARDS**

Open-side flanker
George Smith breaks
clear to score for the
ACT Brumbies against
the Canterbury
Crusaders in the Grand
Final of Super-12 2000
in Canberra. The
Crusaders ran out
narrow winners by 20
points to 19.

After any World Cup there is inevitably change. The season after the World Cup sees changes within the team that wins, as well as obvious changes to the teams that fail to go all the way. For the southern hemisphere nations, the Super-12 season in 2000 was an interesting one. It brought out new talent that will shape the Australian, New Zealand and South African sides that will compete for the William Webb Ellis Trophy in 2003.

The Wallabies were victorious in Cardiff in 1999. They took out the most sacred of rugby silverware, known affectionately Down Under as 'Bill'. The aftermath of Australia's win saw the retirements of prop Andrew Blades and hooker Phil Kearns, as well as the signal that many players who had starred for Australia in the past were now nearing the ends of their careers. Inspirational captain John Eales, centres Tim Horan and Jason Little, and hard-working back-rower David Wilson won't be wearing the gold jersey into the next World Cup, and so a search for replacements has begun.

Whereas Rod Macqueen remains as Wallaby coach, Jeff Miller is no longer the Australian forwards coach (but still remains as a Wallaby selector). Miller's coaching replacement is former Wallaby prop, and 1991 World Cup hero, Ewen McKenzie. Tim Lane remains as Wallaby backs coach but is removed from the panel of Australian selectors because of his new role as backs coach for the NSW Waratahs. The three Wallaby selectors are Macqueen, Miller and former Wallaby captain Andrew Slack.

Rather than opting for wholesale changes, the panel named an initial Wallaby squad for 2000 that reinforced Australia's success in the international arena in 1999. However, the Wallaby selectors did spy some fresh talent. The ACT Brumbies were Australia's shining light in the Super-12 campaign of 2000. They reached the final, losing by just one point to New Zealand's Canterbury Crusaders. The Brumbies played fast, exciting, running rugby and unleashed some highly talented players who are destined for bigger and better things. Stirling Mortlock showed himself to be a strong threequarter with the ability to take the ball over the gain line. His transformation to a feared midfield giant was no coincidence. Mortlock's discipline improved remarkably in the off season; he stepped up his weights training and increased his upper-body strength by 20 per cent. He is a player of damaging ability when confident, and Mortlock's utility status will be an asset to the Wallabies.

Another player in the Brumbies talented back line is Andrew Walker. Walker scored 13 tries in the 2000 Super-12 competition to top the try scorers' list. The 26-year-old may not be well known to international rugby fans, but he is certainly well known in Australia. He was successful in junior Rugby Union but made a name for himself playing Rugby League. He was in the St George Dragons team from 1992 until 1994, and then in the Sydney Roosters side from 1995 to 1999. Walker played one Rugby League Test for Australia against Papua New Guinea in 1996. He now hopes to become a dual international. Walker made his return to the Union code with ease, slotting straight into the star-studded Brumbies back line. In his first Super-12 match, against Auckland, he crossed for two tries, and in his second, against the Sharks, bagged a hat-trick.

NSW Waratahs wing Scott Staniforth launches the ball into touch against the Otago Highlanders.

Walker found himself in the Wallaby shadow squad at the start of the 2000 Test series, along with 19-year-old open-side flanker George Smith. Smith, of Tongan origin, had a meteoric rise to prominence. He was first earmarked as a star in the making when he played in the Australian Schoolboy side in 1997. His timing and his ability to read the play went well beyond his tender years. The tall Brumbies breakaway with trademark dreadlocks takes after David Wilson with his boundless energy and work ethic. Smith scored a try for his ACT side in the Super-12 final in 2000.

A second 19-year-old who found himself part of the Wallabies in 2000 is NSW Waratah back-rower David Lyons. Named on the bench for Australia's first Test of the season against Argentina, Lyons had made a remarkable transition from the Sydney University 1st XV Colts team the year before. Lyons is a powerful open-field runner, standing 6ft 6ins tall and weighing almost 19 stones. This solid youngster was an Australian Schoolboy in 1997 and then skippered the team on their undefeated tour to the United Kingdom in 1998. He was highly sought after by Rugby League scouts but signed with the Waratahs. In 2000 he made his Super-12 debut off the bench against the Stormers and found himself in the starting line-up in round six against Queensland.

Another shining light for the Waratahs in 2000 was open-side flanker Phil Waugh. In 2000 Waugh was named captain of the Australian U21 side because of his mobility and determination and has a bright future in the game. In the backs, 22-year-old winger Scott Staniforth is a fast-improving speedster. Pace and potential earned him a spot as the rookie on the 1998 Wallaby tour to France and England. In 1999 he earned a World Cup trip and a Test debut. One more exciting 22-year-old NSW back is outside centre Luke Inman. Destined to take over from veteran Wallaby Jason Little, Inman is an athletic centre with tremendous ball skills. He was a key member of the Sydney University minor premiership side in 1999 and was rewarded with a prestigious University Blue.

Test rugby in 2000 has seen big changes for the All Blacks. The New Zealand side were the big disappointment of the 1999 World Cup. Most, and especially the Kiwis themselves, expected that the All Blacks would win. When they failed to even make the final it was time for heads to roll. The first casualty was coach John Hart. The new All Black coach was the man who had taken the Canterbury Crusaders to successive Super-12 title wins in 1998 and 1999, Wayne Smith. The new All Black selection panel was Smith, Tony Gilbert and Peter Thorburn.

The next big change was in the player department, starting at captain. When the first New Zealand squad of 2000 was announced, Taine Randell was one of the 26 names, but there was no 'c' beside it. Instead, the man who had just led the Crusaders to their third consecutive Super-12 victory, Todd Blackadder, was made skipper.

Selectors notice players in winning sides, which explains why 11 of the 26 named in the initial All Black squad for 2000 hail from the Christchurch-based outfit. Smith made it clear that form, not reputation, was to be rewarded. The Crusaders' 22-year-old full back Leon MacDonald had a strong Super-12, making breaks, chasing well and displaying outstanding defence. Smith had no qualms about selecting the youngster for higher honours, as he needed a cover for Christian Cullen at full back. While he played in his favoured No. 15 jersey, MacDonald was picked for New Zealand because of his ability to cover so many back-line positions. MacDonald has a rich rugby background as the fifth generation in his family to play first-class rugby in New Zealand. He has earned the right credentials along the way, having played for New Zealand Secondary Schools, U19, Colts and Maori.

Troy Flavell of Auckland Blues dives over for a try as Norm Maxwell of the Crusaders tries in vain to keep him out. Maxwell had the last laugh as the Crusaders went on to win this match at Christchurch by 32 points to 20.

Three provincial team-mates of MacDonald – Mark Robinson, Greg Somerville and Ron Cribb – were also among the newcomers to the Test arena, while other rookies in Smith's first All Black squad were winger Doug Howlett and lock Troy Flavell of the Auckland Blues. Howlett has played for New Zealand U16, Secondary Schools and Colts. He represented the New Zealand U21 side for three years, bagging four tries in the first tournament, six in the second and four in the third. He played his first Super-12 game in 1997, scoring three tries for the Otago Highlanders. Howlett, now 21 years of age, has a fine pedigree, having been educated at the prestigious Auckland Grammar School. He is now continuing his studies at Auckland University. Howlett had an impressive Super-12

series in 2000, standing out in the disorganised Blues back line. His pace makes him a major weapon, although he is also a strong defender and can play at full back. Like MacDonald, he has benefited from the retirement of Jeff Wilson.

A player hardly anyone even knew about at the beginning of 2000 was centre Mark Robinson, but he impressed in a position where New Zealand hardly have great riches. He has a reputation as a thinking centre, something the All Blacks desperately need to unleash the power they have out wide in the form of Lomu, Cullen and Umaga. The 26-year-old, who represented Cambridge University twice in the annual Varsity Match against Oxford, proved a bright spark for the Crusaders in 2000.

One of Robinson's most valuable team-mates was Ron Cribb. Only a few years ago Cribb was living out of an old car and now the No. 8 has a big future as an All Black ahead of him. Originally from North Harbour, Cribb was an Auckland Blues selection in 1999, but injury ruled him out of the squad. In 2000 the Blues didn't want him, so he headed south. He settled into the Crusaders side with ease and put in a brilliant season. Cribb topped off his sizzling season by scoring an opportunist solo try at a crucial time in the 2000 Super-12 final.

Another new forward in the All Black squad comes from Cribb's old turf, in the North Island. Lock Troy Flavell was one of just a handful of Harbour players the Blues picked up in 2000 – and he didn't disappoint. His barnstorming play and abrasive nature made him a crowd favourite, and, like Cribb, he has been earmarked as someone to put the mongrel back in the All Black forward play. Flavell plays with vigour and revels in pushing the laws of the game to the boundaries.

Up front, a big prop named Somerville was another appealing youngster for the Crusaders. At 22 years of age, his performances against much more experienced players at scrum time were strong, as was his work rate around the park. He edged out the likes of Paul Thomson, Gordon Slater and team-mate Greg Feek in what must have been one of the tougher calls of the New Zealand selectors.

Another up-and-coming Kiwi player is Orene Ai'i. While Ai'i is not yet up to All Black selection, he is one to watch for the future. With Carlos Spencer injured for the first half of the Super-12 series in 2000, Ai'i took up the challenge for the Auckland Blues in the No. 10 jersey. Ai'i is a similar style of player to Spencer, with a creative knack for breaking the line. He has amazing skills, is quick, and for a player who is relatively small he is extremely strong. Ai'i is a gifted athlete who has been pivotal to New Zealand sevens success, and at 20 years of age shows a great deal of maturity on the field.

The Springboks managed third place in Rugby World Cup 1999 after pushing the Wallabies to extra time in the semi-final at Twickenham. But the Super-12 has never been a happy hunting ground for the South Africans, who have trouble winning away. In the Springbok squad for 2000, coach Nick Mallett made a conscious effort to blend youth with experience. The squad was made up of ten players aged 25 or under and had an average age of just 26; but the total number of caps at season start was 411.

The Cats were the bright spot for the Republic in the 2000 Super-12 tournament, under the tutelage of former All Black coach Laurie Mains. With Rassie Erasmus injured at the start of the 2000 season, 25-year-old Andre Vos assumed the captaincy of the Cats; he was also made the new skipper of the Springboks. Vos has exceptional leadership skills, having captained practically every side he has played in, and is set to become a first-rate Springbok captain.

Under the direction of Vos and Mains, new young talent was unleashed by the Cats during the 2000 Super-12 season. Two of the Cats backs, Grant Esterhuizen and Louis

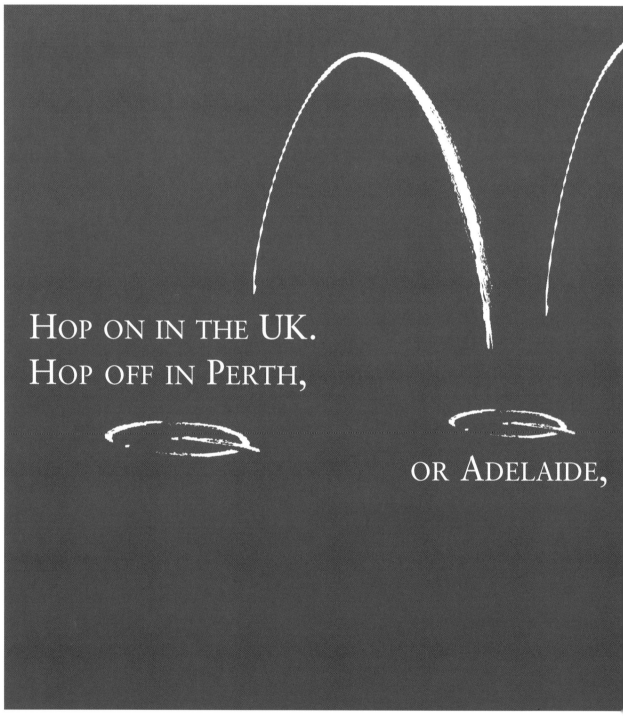

HOP ON IN THE UK.
HOP OFF IN PERTH,

OR ADELAIDE,

Leap on a Cathay Pacific flight to Hong Kong and hop on to any one of our six Australian destinations. We fly three times a day from the UK – and there are 34 flights a week from Hong Kong to Australia, so you can travel when it best suits you. And of

OR CAIRNS,

OR BRISBANE,

OR SYDNEY,

OR MELBOURNE.

...urse, you fly in style, pampered by the legendary Cathay Pacific service. For further
...etails, contact any IATA travel agent or call us on 020 7747 8888. Because when it
...omes to a choice of Australian destinations, we've got the jump on our competition.

Fly Cathay Pacific. The Heart of Asia.

CATHAY PACIFIC

Louis Koen, who plays his Super-12 rugby for the Cats, prepares to kick at goal during the Nelson Mandela Trophy match between South Africa and Australia at Melbourne in July 2000. The Wallabies won this game by 44 points to 23.

Koen, were rewarded for their outstanding play by being named as two of the four new caps included in the first South African squad announced in 2000. Esterhuizen may not be a well-known name in rugby circles, but his commitment to his rugby has been undeniable. The 24-year-old centre moved from the Blue Bulls to the Lions, where he performed brilliantly in the Currie Cup. He then moved on to represent the Cats in the Super-12 competition. He also spent the off season playing for Newport in Wales. Esterhuizen is fast and elusive and very strong in defence. The greatest asset he brings to the Boks is a much-needed element of attack with his line-breaking ability.

One of Esterhuizen's team-mates, Koen also made a big impression in the Super-12. A product of Stellenbosch University, this fly half moved from Western Province after five seasons to link up with the Lions and Cats in order to be noticed. In 2000 Koen helped set the Cats back line alight while remaining an accurate goal-kicker. Another member of the successful Cats back line, Thinus Delport, earned a recall to the Bok squad. He had a brief burst with the national squad in 1997 but was never given a Test berth. Delport played his part for the Cats in 2000, distinguishing himself as their star winger. He showed blistering pace and evasive running along with crowd favourite and fellow winger Chester Williams.

The new South African squad also looked to talented youngsters outside the Cats. Two new caps in the squad of 28 included a pair who had toured together with the victorious South Africa U21 team that won the SANZAR/UAR tournament in Argentina in 1999. The duo are Sharks hooker John Smit, who captained the Colts team, and Stormers centre De Wet Barry. Smit is now 22 years of age and stands out as a front-rower with great potential. He represented the South African Barbarians in 1999 and is now preparing to give his all for the cause of the senior Springbok side when given his chance.

The youngest member of the South African squad for 2000 is De Wet Barry, who is only 21. He comes from the Koue Bokkeveld, the fruit growing area of Ceres in the Boland, as does his Stormers team-mate Breyton Paulse. Barry, who is an old boy of the Paarl Gym Rugby Academy, first pulled on a Springbok jersey beside Robbie Fleck against Canada. Springbok coach Nick Mallett realises that rebuilding is essential, hence these new faces on the fringe of the Bok team. As the cycle towards the 2003 Rugby World Cup begins, the South African selectors know the importance of giving young players a chance. They are also confident that these are players who have the ability to make it at the highest level and they have already proven in the Super-12 that they have what it takes.

SAFARI RUGBY:
RWC Sevens 2001

BY **CHRIS THAU**

Scorers keep the board ticking over at the East Africa Rugby Union ground, Nairobi, during the RWC Sevens qualifier between Uganda and Madagascar.

There was something in the air on Sunday 25 June at the cosy East Africa Rugby Union ground in the centre of Kenya's capital city, Nairobi. The crowd had swelled to about 10,000, an all-time record for the ground. The Kenyan team, who had had a modest build-up on the seeding day, having won two and lost one, suddenly shifted into top gear and found themselves within a step of what the previous day had looked like an impossible dream – a place in the finals of the RWC Sevens.

The colourful cheerleaders and the good-humoured crowd went into overdrive and contributed to the festive atmosphere. Zimbabwe had already qualified, having won 21-0 against the unexpectedly resourceful Tunisia in the first semi-final. It was the turn of the Kenyan boys against the second-favourites, Namibia, in the second semi-final. And then time stopped. Fifteen minutes later, the referee blew full-time and Kenya had made it to the RWC finals for the first time ever. Tears were flowing freely at the end of the historic encounter. 'There is a saying in my language, Luyha: *Omusata nalira esindu silikho* [When a man cries there is something about], and I was not the only one to shed tears,' KRFU Executive Officer Ronal Bukusi said.

For six years, Kenyan rugby has been implementing an ambitious and far-reaching development programme, and the somewhat fortuitous yet still well deserved runner-up position in the tournament is simply a result of the enormous amount of hard work, expertise and resources poured into the project by the KRFU and the IRB. 'It has been a long struggle and taken six years to build a base. We have qualified for RWC and that will do wonders for rugby in this country. Finally, all our investment in time, money (which we seriously lack) and energy paid off. I honestly hope that we will be able to handle the pressure that comes with the territory,' Bukusi added.

'This is wonderful news and a genuine shot in the arm for Kenyan rugby. On the strength of our performance on day one, when we blew hot and cold and looked a bit rusty – we beat both Madagascar and Kazakhstan and lost to our neighbours and archrivals Uganda – I did not think we could make it. To be honest, it was the injury-time defeat by Uganda that enabled us to avoid Zimbabwe in the semi-finals, which would have probably changed the outcome of the tournament. Having said that, the boys took their chances with both hands and credit to them and coach Bill Githinji. The team played increasingly well on day two and showed their true potential by finishing second to the very powerful Zimbabwe team,' Stuart Urquhart, Kenyan Team Manager and KRFU Development Officer, said.

The quiet satisfaction of the former Scottish Students and England Schools wing forward was obvious. The overall success of Kenyan teams in the tournament – the runner-up position for the senior side, and victory for the seconds, the Shujaas (Warriors), in the parallel Safari Sevens Tournament the day before – gives a fair idea of the robust health of Kenyan rugby and its considerable potential.

Unquestionably, Safari Sevens, held yearly since 1996, has had a considerable impact on Kenyan and East African rugby, which is deprived of regular international competition other than the four-yearly RWC. Launched in 1996 by a group of enthusiasts, who still run it with clockwork precision and great management skills, Safari Sevens has offered Kenya, and East African rugby a stage on which to express their international ambitions. The tournament, one of the most prestigious in Africa, is held at the historically famous East Africa RFU ground, host to many touring sides, including Dr Craven's Stellenbosch University in 1935 and the 1955 British Lions.

Above: A Kenyan fan gets in the spirit. The qualification of the Kenyan team for the RWC finals was an emotional event and 'a genuine shot in the arm for Kenyan rugby'.
Right: Botswana (blue and black) take on Tunisia.

However, while Safari Sevens has provided the missing international dimension, it is the work of the likes of Urquhart and Bukusi that brought about the change in fortunes of Kenyan rugby. Driven by these two, the game is experiencing a real upsurge in the rural regions, previously no-go areas for rugby. The pair have targeted schools and universities in the west and northwest of the country and the results have been astonishing.

Says Urquhart, a hard-working, unsmiling Scot who commenced his career as a rugby developer with the first RFU Development Team: 'In three years, over 150 schools in the rural areas of the country, mostly in the west and northwest, have commenced playing rugby. Obviously we are hampered by a lack of resources and finance, but even so, the support we receive from the IRB, who are actually funding my job attachment with the KRFU, has helped us to make ends meet.

'The best marketing tool in rugby is the ball, and we don't have enough of those to leave behind. However, as a result of our intensive development programme there has been a marked change of scenery in Kenyan youth and schools rugby, with the centre of gravity moving from Nairobi's traditional rugby schools – Lenana, St Mary's, or Nairobi College – to schools in the west and northwest – Kakamega, St Mary Yala, Masena, Mangu, Malindi, Kilifi, you name it.'

Safari Sevens has acted as a catalyst for several of the East African nations, including Uganda, Zambia and Madagascar, who impressed the pundits with their genuine potential. Interestingly enough, the presence of two lowly placed teams from Asia and Europe – Kazakhstan and Bosnia respectively – has given African rugby some sort of yardstick with which to compare its average quality with that of foreign opposition. If Botswana and Swaziland are, judged by the table of the 12-team event, at the bottom of the African heap, they are clearly superior to the overseas visitors. Botswana, who won the Bowl, beat Kazakhstan 38-7, while Swaziland desfeated Bosnia 49-0. The exposure will offer nations such as Kenya, Zambia, Uganda and Madagascar the missing international dimension, and sevens will allow them to fully express their huge potential. 'The quality displayed by several African countries defies their resources and is very heartening. There is a sense of optimism among all African nations as we prepare to launch the second and third tier of the continental competition, aimed at kick-starting the game in the member unions,' Chairman of the Confederation of African Rugby Dr Hamda Belkiria said.

A Zambian defender clings on to a Côte d'Ivoire opponent, forcing him to look around for support. Says the Zambian coach of the country's rugby potential, 'With the right resources, the sky is the limit.'

Uganda, one of the newer members of the IRB, have been developing – with the help of their friends, neighbours and main adversaries, Kenya – a sound infrastructure, and in true rugby fashion have been giving their 'rugby masters' a hard time. Coached by former Kenyan scrum half Tolbert Onayngo, Uganda beat their neighbours and friends 17-14 on day one, thanks to a giant dropped goal in injury time by Uganda's inspirational captain, Herbert Wafula – a supreme act of rugby opportunism and intelligence.

If Zambia is used as a sample to judge the progress of the game in Africa during an RWC cycle, then the progress is indeed astonishing. They used to say that sevens is the game in which you cannot hide. It reveals technical shortcomings and tactical naivety with the same ruthlessness as it exposes talent and ability. If Zambia, who finished the competition in eighth position – equal with Madagascar, one of the surprise packs of the two-day event – represent the current standard of African rugby, then the African rugby revolution has commenced.

Zambia, one of Africa's many developing unions, full of human potential yet painfully short of resources, hit the international scene in the qualifying rounds of the previous RWC Sevens. The team was coached by the late Sam Tembo, one of the pioneers of Zambian rugby, but the skill and comprehension of Zambian players failed to match their obvious enthusiasm and athleticism. Subsequently, Zambia entered the qualifying rounds of RWC 1999 and competed manfully against Botswana and Arabian Gulf; this was their only international competition in the last five years.

Participation in RWC, the lure of the big rugby scene and the potential of professional contracts must have had a dramatic impact on Zambian rugby and its structure. The quality displayed on day one against Namibia, who managed to eventually draw level in the dying moments of an exciting game Zambia should have won, defies Zambia's low ranking among the African nations. Moreover, Zambia had not come to Nairobi to win the tournament, although they achieved a great deal of exposure to international competition by entering their seconds in the Safari Sevens. They were there, observed the Zambian coach, Musa Zimba, to make a statement about the aspirations and enormous potential of Zambian rugby: 'With the right resources, the sky is the limit,' Zimba said.

Meanwhile, in the final of the first European qualifying zone tournament in Heidelberg, Germany, one would have found it quite difficult to distinguish between winners and losers at the end of an exciting, at times dramatic, final, such was the joy of both finalists, Wales and Georgia, at the end of it. Wales, skippered by Cardiff utility back-rower and sevens specialist Owain Williams, finished unbeaten, to win their first ever major sevens tournament, while Georgia had been celebrating their coming of age as a rugby nation.

It was both the achievement in itself and the swashbuckling style that gave Williams, Thomas, Morgan and Co reasons to celebrate. On the other hand, Georgia's mild disappointment at

Arwel Thomas (left) and Kevin Morgan of Wales show off the silverware they won in the first European qualifying zone tournament at Heidelberg. The pair were top points scorer and top try scorer respectively.

losing the final was overwhelmed by the joy of joining Wales and bronze medallists Ireland in the finals of the RWC Sevens in Mar del Plata, Argentina – they are the first ever Georgian team to reach the finals of a world event.

In the second European tournament in Madrid, the Russians and the Spanish between them were guilty of the ultimate sevens rugby indignity, when they eliminated Scotland, the inventors of the short game, from the third RWC Sevens. Portugal, Russia and Spain qualified for Mar del Plata at the end of two days of sizzling rugby action in the scorching Madrid sun.

Earlier, at the end of the two-tier Americas qualifying process, Canada, one of the new forces of the IRB Sevens Series circuit, confirmed their favourite status by winning the Santiago tournament, although Chile, the surprise item of the Americas, gave them a fright in the final. From the outset, it was clear that besides Canada only two of the chasing pack of the USA, Chile, Trinidad and Tobago, and Uruguay would make it to Mar del Plata 2001. Who was going to fail in the race for those remaining two positions was always a matter for some speculation, but when first Trinidad and Tobago and then eventually Uruguay fell by the wayside, the public seemed unperturbed. However, the 6,000-odd spectators went positively wild when – perhaps to convince everybody that they should believe in fairy tales – the Chilean Condors beat archrivals Uruguay to book a place in the 2001 finals, the first time a Chilean rugby team had reached the final of an RWC tournament.

In Asia, though, there was very little the new, aspiring nations, with the exception of the increasingly assertive People's Republic of China, could do to prevent the sevens troika of Japan, Chinese Taipei and Korea from winning the Asian leg of the Mar del Plata RWC Sevens Tournament. The 24th finalist in Mar del Plata will be announced at the end of the final qualifying tournament for the Pacific zone in Raratonga in September.

The Georgian squad that qualified at Heidelberg for the RWC Sevens finals at Mar del Plata, Argentina, becoming in the process the first Georgian side to reach the finals of a world event.

SCOTTISH AMICABLE AND THE BARBARIANS: FOR TEN YEARS WE'VE BEEN A FORMIDABLE TEAM

THE SCOTTISH AMICABLE TOUR: A GREAT END TO THE SEASON.

Through our continuing sponsorship of the Barbarians, we bring together the best of the world's rugby talent to do battle in front of home fans. In 2001 the Barbarians are back with more great games for you to enjoy. So watch out for the Barbarians' end of season Scottish Amicable Tour and prepare to be thrilled.

Scottish Amicable
TOUR

www.scottishamicable.co.uk

NOT JUST A SCOTTISH AND AMICABLE TOUR: the Barbarians in 2000

BY NIGEL STARMER-SMITH

It was an ambitious undertaking, but one which marked a genuine rejuvenation and, in part, a restoration of the status of the Barbarian Football Club. For more than 100 years the Barbarians epitomised the very best of rugby for players and spectators alike. However, as one of the casualties of the new, and in many ways destructive, era of professionalism, the BaaBaas had been left by the wayside. The old-style Corinthian ethos of this unique touring club – true amateurism; the camaraderie, fun and frolics off the field and on it on the Easter tour of South Wales; and the accolade of the invitation to wear the famous black-and-white jersey which ranked second only to that of one's country or the British Lions – all that may have gone forever. Yet to the lasting credit of those who remain at the helm of the BaaBaas – in particular their president, Mickey Steele-Bodger, and his committee – they have managed through their determination and pragmatism to keep the flame alive. In an era of ten-month, overcrowded seasons, World Cups, full-time professional squads contracted to club and country, the light of Barbarian rugby, with 'attack' as its watchword, could so readily have been extinguished. So it was with considerable relief that the BaaBaas were able to step onto the international stage once more – with the co-operation of the Irish, Scottish and English rugby unions, of the clubs and ten nations who released their players to take part, and, not least, of Scottish Amicable, whose generosity as the Barbarians' sole sponsor over the past ten years ultimately transformed a possibility into a reality.

The opening encounter of the Scottish Amicable three-match tour took place at Lansdowne Road on Sunday 28 May as the focal point of the celebrations of the 125th anniversary of the IRFU. Anyone who thought we might be in for a half-hearted end-of-season friendly exhibition was swiftly disabused, but a glance down the list of names in the Barbarian squad would have given the lie to any such notions anyway. Drawn from

Barbarians skipper-for-the-day Zinzan Brooke on the rampage against Leicester in the Scottish Amicable Trophy match at Twickenham. The 35-year-old Brooke, playing his last first-class game, scored one of the BaaBaas 13 tries in their 85-10 victory.

Lomu on the loose at Lansdowne Road. The BaaBaas shaded this very physical contest 32-31 against a determined Ireland side that lost three members of its summer touring party to injury during the game.

ten nations, the squad was a true assembly of world-class talent, as Lomu, Little and Dowd of New Zealand, Muller, Terblanche, le Roux and Dalton of South Africa, Puma Pichot and Wallaby Morgan took the field. In fact the game was a bruising – and for Ireland a costly – contest. In a very physical, closely fought match, Ireland were to lose three of the party due to depart on their American tour the following day: Brian O'Driscoll, Girvan Dempsey and Geordan Murphy. Two others required hospital treatment but were still able to travel to Argentina.

Given the catalogue of injuries, Ireland did remarkably well to confine the illustrious Barbarians to a one-point victory. The courage and dogged defence was no less than heroic. Kevin Maggs marshalled Jonah Lomu from start to finish and Guy Easterby had a glorious debut at scrum half, and each scored one of Ireland's four tries, the others coming from Shane Horgan and Justin Bishop. Behind at half-time, the Barbarians came back with tries by Agustin Pichot (what a player!) and two from Stefan Terblanche. In fact, had captain-for-the-day David Humphreys succeeded with an injury-time penalty goal attempt, Ireland would have denied the Barbarians their hard-earned victory, which they eventually gained by 32 points to 31. For Ireland, it was, literally, a very painful defeat!

Three days later, Scotland chose to award full caps for their Wednesday evening encounter with the Barbarians at Murrayfield to mark the 75th anniversary of the ground. After the proceedings in Dublin, the BaaBaas coach Bob Dwyer hardly needed to emphasise in the pre-match press conference in Edinburgh his aspirations for the team. 'We don't want to have a mock game of pretend rugby. Crowds know when things are not for real.' Do they ever! And was there ever any chance of that with the two All Black Brooke brothers, Robin and Zinzan, Scott Gibbs, Viliame Satala, Joeli Vidiri, and England's Luger, Leonard and Dallaglio? The end result was a real game and real entertainment in the best of the club's tradition. A crowd of almost 30,000 revelled in another nail-biting finish, as Scotland roared back in a great second-half revival before losing by 42 points to 45.

England wing Dan Luger, fresh back from a long injury lay-off, rounds Scotland's Chris Paterson on the way to the try line. The Barbarians seemed to be cruising to victory in this middle fixture of their tour, but a second-half fightback by the Scots brought the final score to 45-42.

Two tries by Dan Luger, another by Matt Perry, and two more by the irrepressible All Black Vidiri had hinted at a mauling for the Scots. Not a bit of it! A Richard Metcalfe try and penalty goals by Duncan Hodge kept hopes alive for the home team, before a second-half blitz by Scotland that put a broad smile on coach Ian McGeechan's formerly furrowed face. Two tries by Graham Shiel, who starred on his return to the international fold, and one each for Gordon Bulloch and Hodge brought a fitting climax – before Munster hero John Langford and, appropriately, Vidiri added the Barbarians' winning tries and the coup de grâce. The next day Scotland flew off on tour to New Zealand in fine fettle – and, unlike Ireland, minus only the one injured player, Jamie McLaren.

Without doubt, those two first-class matches overshadowed what was to follow. Sadly the festive farewell to the interminable domestic season, and the final match of the Scottish Amicable tour, was almost bound to be something of an anticlimax, pitching as

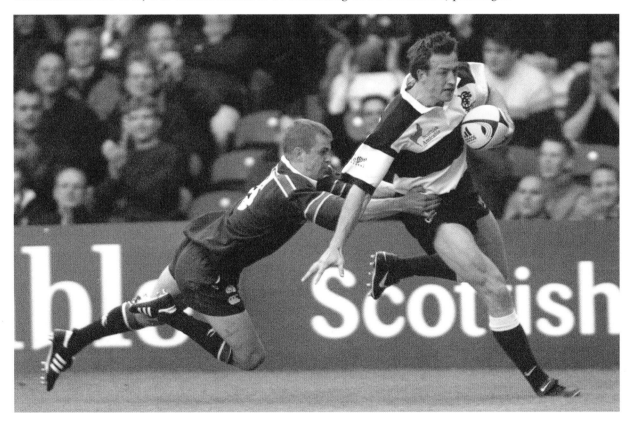

it did a valiant but jaded club side against yet another world-class Barbarian combination. Leicester have long cherished their close ties with the BaaBaas – their annual fixture began as the Christmas Holiday highlight back in 1909. By happy coincidence the meeting this year took place at Twickenham, Leicester having won the honour of fulfilling this fixture as the champions, again, of the Allied Dunbar Premiership. It proved to be a game too far for Martin Johnson's wilting Tigers at the tail end of what, for the bulk of his team, had been an exhausting season of league, cup, European and international rugby. For six of the Leicester squad, there was also the little matter of an England tour to South Africa in the offing. Facing the Tigers in front of a 50,000 crowd – and bear in mind how determined and committed are southern hemisphere players by their very nature – was the entire Springbok front row, All Black lock forwards Robin Brooke and Ian Jones, plus Lawrence Dallaglio, Ruben Kruger, and (playing his final first-class game at age 35) captain-for-the-day Zinzan Brooke. With Rob Howley and Neil Jenkins, Vidiri, Walter Little, Luger and more, the Barbarians were not likely to let their leader down on his farewell appearance, especially in front of his parents, who had flown over specially!

Yet the star of the show was not one of that list but the new Barbarian recruit for this match – the smallest man on the field, playing at full back. Providing the most wonderful moments of Barbarian virtuosity, in the best traditions of the club, was Thomas Castaignède, with two first-half tries born of 60 and 70 yards of magical running. Saracens supporters must have been salivating at the prospect of seeing him in their club jersey next season.

Two-try Thomas Castaignède tears upfield against Leicester. The Frenchman, playing at full back for the Barbarians, comes to Saracens next season.

Suffice to say, Leicester were brave to the last but outgunned throughout. Thirteen Barbarian tries (including, appropriately, one by Zinzan, cheered to the echo) to two by Leicester says it all – 85 points to 10 was an unsurprising scoreline under these particular circumstances. Never mind. The tour put the Barbarians back on the road and back on the map. And, with all those tries, just think how youth rugby has benefited, with £300 a score being donated by Scottish Amicable to that worthy cause. Since Scottish Amicable started the scheme, the total amount donated by them has risen to £123,300 in the 'Amicable Gesture'! At least somewhere in the realms of rugby the money is being well spent.

The author is the Official Historian of Barbarian F.C.

UNSTOPPABLE MOMENTUM: the World Junior Championship

BY **CHRIS THAU**

There is an unstoppable momentum to all this. From the humble beginnings of the first tournament, held in 1969, the World Junior (U19) Championship has gone from strength to strength and established itself as the premier youth competition in the world – 2000 was its 32nd year. New Zealand having entered for the first time in 1999, Australia, Samoa, Tonga and Korea this year joined the glittering cast of the streamlined 32-nation competition, hosted by two of France's most ambitious rugby committees – Franche-Comté and Burgundy. The two finals – Australia v France in Division One and Samoa v Korea in Division Two – involved three of the four newcomers and are a testament to the meritocratic nature of the competition.

'For me, all this has a special flavour and gives me great satisfaction. I have been involved with this tournament since its early days, first as coach of the French [U19] juniors, then as an FFR organiser, and finally, as part of the FIRA-AER organisation, as one of the people responsible for its safe delivery. To say that I feel personally vindicated by its enormous success is an understatement. There have been many doubting Thomases, who questioned the value and the role of the tournament. But we kept our heads down and battled to develop it to its current status and magnitude,' FIRA-AER President Jean-Claude Baque said.

Action from the Tonga v Korea semi-final in the World Junior Championship second division. The Koreans prevailed to meet Samoa in the final.

Georgia dominate the line out against Paraguay.

The fact that both France and Australia reached their second consecutive world championship final (following RWC 1999) was not a coincidence and suggested that both unions, in addition to their elite programmes, have been equally busy nurturing their grass-root schemes. Last year's finalists, New Zealand and Wales, had to content themselves with the bronze medal play-off, but their consistency also suggests development programmes of the highest calibre. The Welsh have been regularly present in the final stages of the competition since they joined five years ago, and the New Zealanders have won a gold and a bronze in two appearances.

However, although winning is important, and without it the very essence of healthy sporting competition is undermined, the IRB/FIRA-AER World Junior Championship is more about development, and this is something the more emotional team managers, coaches and, surprisingly, team doctors may wish to reflect upon.

'It is essential to understand that winning, while an intrinsic part of sporting competition and the sporting ethic, is not the ultimate objective of this event. Playing well and winning in that order is what we are after,' FIRA-AER Director of Development Robert Antonin observed.

This is a somewhat distant, yet refreshing, reminder of the old and probably forgotten Olympic motto often paraphrased to 'taking part is more important than winning'. Well, try saying that to a 19-year-old John Eales lookalike, one Daniel Heenan, lock forward and captain of the young Wallabies, who was seemingly unable to understand why the 6 November 1999 scenario, when the Wallabies blitzed the French into silver medal position at Cardiff, failed to replicate itself in Dijon at the end of a stupendous game that matched the intensity and quality of the senior final. The simplest and perhaps most obvious answer to why the outcome was different is probably the overall quality of the French team, their remarkable fitness and the nearly perfect organisation of their defence masterminded by two unassuming yet very competent coaches, Bernard Charreyere and Michel Lazergef.

'There was nothing special about this French team. They are very good players, and we have plenty of those in France. There were a few outstanding characters among them, but by and large the secret of our success was simply work, a lot of it and most of it of very, very high quality and intensity,' Charreyere said.

However, it is obvious that trying to instil the 'winning at any cost' mentality at this age is both dangerous and could be counterproductive in both the medium and long term. There is no more competitive sporting individual than an Australian athlete, yet the admirable dignity in defeat of the young Wallabies, managed by an exceptionally calm and composed Ron Dwyer and coached by Gary Ella and David Cater, was as impressive as the low-key joy of the drained French youngsters. In the lower division, the Samoan teenagers – on their first ever trip outside Samoa – played some magnificent rugby, according to their manager, impressing the public and, more significantly, gaining their country promotion to Division One for next year's event in Chile.

The Samoan captain receives the second division trophy after his side beat Korea in the final. On the left of the picture is IRB President Vernon Pugh.

Arguably, the unique value of this event is its yearly cycle, which enables virtually the entire IRB membership to set in place meaningful domestic developmental programmes for juniors. In the majority of the participating countries, where rugby is a minority game battling to survive in an often hostile economic and sporting climate, the annual process that ends with the World Junior Championship is the lifeblood of their domestic game. It involves hundreds, perhaps thousands of youngsters, and is what gives development both sense and meaning. The competition's yearly cycle provides the domestic structure of these countries with a focus for producing the much-needed players, referees, qualified supporters, and administrators for the senior game. Within this context, the competition itself, with its moments of drama and emotion, skill and passion, is simply a bonus, and ultimately acts as a major promotional tool for the game. Since it was launched 32 years ago, the IRB/FIRA-AER World Junior Championship has become if not the most significant then one of the main developmental programmes in rugby.

'The revival of the game in Chile has a lot to do with the admission of our youth team into the World Junior Championship. The game had been stagnant for some years. The arrival of the RWC has helped our players to focus, but the great impact on numbers

Clash of the titans. The Australian and French front rows prepare to mix it in the first division final. France ran out winners to prevent a Wallaby world championship double.

and awareness was the IRB/FIRA-AER World Junior Championship. The stars of the Chilean team of today are the players who represented Chile in the IRB/FIRA tournament a few years ago,' said Miguel Mujica Brain, the President of the Chile Rugby Federation. A few weeks later, Chile, the hosts of the 33rd IRB/FIRA-AER World Junior Championship, succeeded in qualifying for the RWC 2001 Sevens finals, fielding a side selected almost entirely from former participants in the World Junior Championship.

While the format of the week-long competition remains the same, the cast is different each year. The format of the competition is designed to make it fit within the time available – the Easter break, which pretty much coincides with school holidays throughout the world. It has been argued that the knock-out system employed, which is very much in line with the Hong Kong pattern of cup, plate and bowl, is too harsh for the teams who fall at the first hurdle. In other words, if a team loses the first match, they plunge to the bottom half of the table (places 9-16), while a win in round one elevates a team to the top eight. The format is far from perfect, and the organisers are well aware of its limitations. However, it is the only system that guarantees the participating teams three to four matches within a week, and unless someone puts forward a suitable alternative, the current format, imperfect perhaps, is likely to stay in place for the forseeable future.

SCOTTISH AMICABLE HALL OF FAME

BY KEVIN STEWART

The second Scottish Amicable International Rugby Hall of Fame Induction Dinner was held in the Great Room of London's Grosvenor House Hotel, with over 700 guests attending another glittering occasion. The evening was hosted in conjunction with the Wooden Spoon Society and the Professional Rugby Players Association (PRA). It was fitting that so many famous players, past and present, were able to attend the dinner, it being held just before the World Cup semi-finals.

The first induction ceremony, in December 1997, also took place in London and saw 15 legends of the game become the inaugural inductees. Of the first XV, Gareth Edwards, Mike Gibson, Barry John, Cliff Morgan, Hugo Porta, Willie-John McBride, and J.P.R. Williams were on hand to welcome the new inductees to the Hall of Fame with the presentation of a specially commissioned limited-edition print. Unfortunately other commitments prevented Tony O'Reilly, Frik du Preez, Serge Blanco, Jean-Pierre Rives, Mark Ella and Colin Meads returning. The late Danie Craven and George Nepia completed the original line-up.

A remarkable gathering of rugby talent. L to r: Gerald Davies, Morne Du Plessis, Andy Irvine, Jack Kyle, Brian Lochore, Mike Gibson, Philippe Sella, Gareth Edwards, Cliff Morgan, JPR Williams, Hugo Porta, Willie-John McBride and Barry John.

Right: Andy Irvine becomes the first Scot to join the Hall of Famers. He is seen here receiving his commemorative print from John Cowan, Sales Director of Scottish Amicable. Below: Two of the greatest centres ever to have graced the game of rugby – Mike Gibson of Ireland and Philippe Sella of France.

Having flown the new inductees in from around the world, it was gratifying to see how many old friends were reunited by the ceremony and how quickly new friends were made across the generations. In 1997, old foes brought together again included Willie-John McBride, Frik du Preez and Colin Meads; this time around, new friendships struck up included the mutual appreciation society formed before the dinner by Philippe Sella, Mike Gibson and Jack Kyle!

The International Hall of Fame sets out to record and acknowledge the impact great players have made on the world stage, drawing on a distinguished panel of 50 international rugby writers and commentators, who are asked to provide their nominations. A nominee must have been retired from international rugby for three years and receive 75 per cent of the vote from the Trustees – one from each of the major rugby-playing nations – before he can be inducted into the Hall of Fame. Those inducted into the Hall of Fame on this special rugby evening were:

Andy Irvine (Scotland)
Jack Kyle (Ireland)
Wavell Wakefield (England)
Brian Lochore (New Zealand)
Wilson Whineray (New Zealand)
Carwyn James (Wales)
Nick Farr-Jones (Australia)
Philippe Sella (France)
Morne Du Plessis (South Africa)
Gerald Davies (Wales)

Each of the attending inductees spoke eloquently of his love of the game, with Wilson Whineray and Nick Farr-Jones, both unable to be there in person, appearing on video. The common themes running through the speeches were genuine appreciation and humility at being honoured amongst such an august group of players – many of the inductees having been inspired by those whom they now stood alongside – and the hope that the professional game would still allow the players to enjoy their rugby, making friendships around the globe that lasted a lifetime.

BBC Sport once again trawled their archives for the magic moments that reminded us why these rugby greats had been elected. Our thanks to them and to Scottish Amicable for sponsoring the event for the second time, building on their support of rugby's best traditions and legends – they also sponsor the Barbarian Rugby Club. Their guests had a night to remember, and we hope the support continues at future induction dinners.

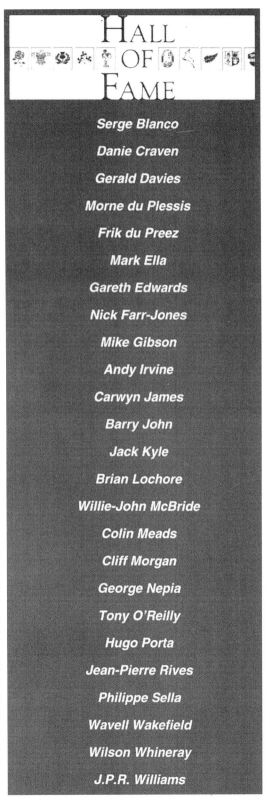

HALL OF FAME

Serge Blanco

Danie Craven

Gerald Davies

Morne du Plessis

Frik du Preez

Mark Ella

Gareth Edwards

Nick Farr-Jones

Mike Gibson

Andy Irvine

Carwyn James

Barry John

Jack Kyle

Brian Lochore

Willie-John McBride

Colin Meads

Cliff Morgan

George Nepia

Tony O'Reilly

Hugo Porta

Jean-Pierre Rives

Philippe Sella

Wavell Wakefield

Wilson Whineray

J.P.R. Williams

Scottish Amicable

HONOURING PLAYERS IN A CLASS OF THEIR OWN

INTERNATIONAL RUGBY

HALL OF FAME

SUMMER TOURS

ENGLAND IN SOUTH AFRICA

BY IAN ROBERTSON

Throughout the last decade of the last century, England's rugby players tended to travel more in hope than expectation. It was not always a disaster, but there was certainly only a rare oasis to enjoy in a fairly barren desert of depressing defeats. They never experienced a single victory against the Wallabies in Australia in nine attempts over a period of 37 years and it was almost the same story in New Zealand, where in 37 years they had just one win against the All Blacks in 1973. They did not fare much better in South Africa where they lost heavily in 1994 in Cape Town, and although in the 1995 World Cup they did have the huge satisfaction of beating Australia in the quarter-finals they were then embarrassingly swept aside by New Zealand in the semi-finals and then beaten by France in the third-place play-off.

The one major success in ten years of Tests against New Zealand, Australia and South Africa in the southern hemisphere came in Pretoria in 1994. On 17 June 2000, England faced South Africa again in Pretoria and they had every reason to go into the match full of optimism. They were, after all, the undisputed Six Nations Champions. Had they not discovered a giant tartan banana skin at Murrayfield on the first Sunday in April they would have landed in South Africa as the Grand Slam Champions of Europe. The English forwards have been pretty formidable throughout the past ten years. Right now

Up go the arms in elation at the final whistle in Bloemfontein, where England beat South Africa by 27 points to 22. This victory in the second Test tied the two-match series and was no more than England deserved after impressive performances in both internationals.

they have not only the best back five forwards in Europe but I doubt that at any time in the past ten years any side could have had a better loose-forward trio than Lawrence Dallaglio, Richard Hill and Neil Back or a much better lock combination than Martin Johnson and Danny Grewcock.

The backs have looked solid in defence in recent seasons but have not looked nearly as threatening in attack as the big guns of the southern hemisphere. However, in the new Millennium all that seems to be changing. Two top-class scrum halves have taken centre stage in Kyran Bracken and Matt Dawson. At long last they have a natural successor to Rob Andrew at fly half in Jonny Wilkinson. Wilkinson is still in the first flush of youth, but he is already a seasoned international player. He was stunningly good in the Bloemfontein Test. Mike Tindall has settled in at Test level as a centre very quickly and he has been helped and cushioned by his Bath colleague Mike Catt, who has a wealth of

Springbok full back Percy Montgomery hurries to help as wing Pieter Rossouw is wrapped up by England's Mike Catt and Neil Back in the second Test at Bloemfontein. The whole England side excelled in defence in this match.

international experience. On the wings England have Austin Healey and Dan Luger, and in Matt Perry an exciting running full back of the highest quality to complete a very good back division. In direct comparison with the Springboks there seemed little doubt that England had the edge and there seemed no reason why England should not enjoy a successful five-match tour. The three midweek matches served their purpose. The second layer of potential England internationals were given their chance and they showed that England had plenty of strength in depth as they proceeded to win all three games. Of course these results were welcomed in the England camp and were very encouraging for the future, but the two games which really mattered were the two Tests.

The first Test in Pretoria will be remembered for all sorts of reasons but mainly because England lost a match they deserved to win. The Springboks admitted afterwards that they were surprised at the fierce commitment, abrasive tackling and outstanding control and organisation of the English team and they conceded that England had made enormous strides since their big World Cup quarter-final defeat by South Africa in Paris.

The game turned on two controversial incidents and both went against England. The first took place 20 minutes into the second half with the score 15-10 to South Africa. Tim Stimpson chased a kick to the goal line and he was in the very act of gaining control of the bouncing ball above his head with his right hand when he was tackled by the Springbok captain Andre Vos. The force of the tackle resulted in Stimpson losing control of the ball and knocking it forward, although he claimed after the match that when the ball landed he still managed to exert downward pressure on it. The evidence of that was not conclusive, but the English squad felt that Stimpson had been tackled over the try line without the ball and a penalty try should have been awarded. At first glance in the heat of the drama they appeared to have a very good case, and without having recourse

England hooker Phil Greening launches a kick-and-chase at the Free State Stadium, Bloemfontein. Kyran Bracken and Ben Cohen lend support as Springbok flanker Andre Venter turns to backtrack.

to the replay which allowed the video referee to make the final decision there is every likelihood the match referee, Colin Hawke of New Zealand, would indeed have awarded a penalty try. Seven points then would almost certainly have led to an England victory. Instead, after a great deal of deliberation, the video referee, Mark Lawrence of South Africa, decided against the penalty try and against a penalty and advised Colin Hawke to award a scrum. It had to be a desperately close decision and it was hard not to feel sorry for England.

The other controversial incident occurred near the end of the match when Leon Lloyd was penalised for retaliating when he was being jostled off the ball. Braam van Straaten kicked the goal to increase the South African lead from 15-13 to 18-13. That was hugely significant. England were awarded half a dozen penalties in the final minutes of the match and had the score been 15-13 and had they kicked any single one of the six penalties they would probably have won the Test. They opted instead not to kick for goal because they trailed by five points and by failing to score a try the match slipped out of their grasp. Nevertheless, it was still an excellent English performance in the circumstances, and it convinced everyone that England had closed the gap with South Africa and they were at least as good and probably a bit better than the Springboks.

The proof came the following Saturday in Bloemfontein when England won the second Test in commanding fashion. This was arguably England's best performance of the entire season. The whole side played superbly, both individually and as a team. The forwards had the edge in every aspect of play and the aggressive defence of the team was quite remarkable. Admittedly they were helped by having Jonny Wilkinson fit to play at fly half after missing the first Test. He and Kyran Bracken were in top form at half back. Furthermore, Wilkinson kicked his goals. He struck eight superb penalties and dropped a goal. He was without doubt the hero of the match. Ironically, in each Test, the only try of the match was scored by the losing side. Dan Luger scored for England in the first Test; Joost van der Westhuizen scored for South Africa in the second Test with the help of the video referee – Andre Watson of South Africa. As each video referee decision in the two Tests was given by a South African referee and each went against England, a strong case will be made in the future for the video referee to be from a neutral country.

In Bloemfontein the only try came from a scrum near the English line in which it looked impossible to determine exactly what happened. The match referee, Stuart Dickinson from Australia, consulted the video referee. After a lengthy examination of the replay, Andre Watson advised Dickinson that van der Westhuizen had touched down over the line for a try. The English argument was that even though that may have been the case a couple of English players had grounded the ball before him. A try should not have been awarded. In the end it didn't matter because England were in control and went on to record one of their most impressive victories of the past decade.

They now really do have the basis of a very good squad and can build for a brighter future. They no longer need to fear the might of South Africa, Australia and New Zealand. In the summer of 2000 they went a long way to closing the gap with the southern hemisphere. They are definitely progressing rapidly in the right direction and if they can achieve consistency of performance they could well be a major force come the next World Cup.

Jonny Wilkinson releases before Joost van der Westhuizen can reach him. Wilkinson had a towering game at Bloemfontein, while the South African scrum half scored the game's only try, a controversial affair that required a ruling from the video referee.

SCOTLAND IN NEW ZEALAND

BY ALAN LORIMER

Few Scotland fans will need reminding that the national team has never beaten New Zealand in almost one hundred years of Test rugby between the two countries. It was an historical fact embedded in the psyche of the Scotland tour party when they set off for their summer tour of New Zealand in early June. It remained unaltered when Scotland returned back home a month later. There is something of a ritualistic annual slaughter when home union countries travel to the Land of the Long White Cloud on so-called summer tours. England suffered a humiliation, albeit with a scratch squad, when they toured in 1998. Two years later Scotland, without the defence of fielding a second team, were soundly defeated in both Tests, the 69-20 drubbing in Dunedin rewriting the record books.

On the face of it, a tour to New Zealand at the end of a protracted club season which had included an exhausting World Cup campaign might have seemed sheer folly. The results from the seven-match visit might endorse that view, but as Ian McGeechan insisted after the second Test against New Zealand, much had been gained in developmental terms. 'We've taken a group of players further forward than they were five weeks ago, and the tour has exposed to New Zealand rugby a number of exciting new players,' said McGeechan. Every national coach in McGeechan's situation might have said that, but the key difference for Scotland is that because of the desperately small number of players in the Scotland set-up those developed on tour are very likely to appear at national level soon afterwards.

Scotland added six new players to their cap list – Ross Beattie and Iain Fullarton in the first Test; Jon Petrie, Steve Scott, Nathan Hines and Graeme Beveridge in the second Test. The competition for the No. 8 position between Beattie and Petrie should prove to be interesting this season. Beattie, 22 when he was first capped, has height, weight and the experience of mixing it in the English first division with Newcastle, while Petrie, a full back up to U19 level, has developed enormously in the Glasgow Caledonians set-up under coach Richie Dixon, winning Scotland A honours before being selected for the tour. Beattie was played in the first Test, but such was the thin line dividing the two that the Scotland coaches opted to play Petrie a week later in the second encounter at Eden Park. The clever move by the coaches was to bring on Beattie for Petrie in the last quarter of the latter game, thus giving the right message to both players.

Of the other new caps to burst into front-line contention, Graeme Beveridge, the Glasgow Caledonians scrum half, looked impressive on tour. The rise to the top for

All Black wing Jonah Lomu hands off Scotland's Cameron Murray during the second Test at Eden Park, Auckland, which New Zealand won 48-14.

BEHIND SCOTTISH RUGBY.

THE FAMOU GROUS
SCOTLAND TEAM SPO

Beveridge has been timely for Scotland in the post-Armstrong period. For Beveridge it was the reward for patience at the end of a frustrating season in which injury ensured only a limited amount of rugby and in which he had to understudy the Scotland captain, Andy Nicol, at Glasgow Caledonians. The strongly built Beveridge, another in the long line of Border scrum halves, has a sharp service and a high work rate round the base of the scrum – ideal for the kind of game McGeechan is inculcating in his players.

Scotland went on tour without Stuart Grimes, whose Newcastle clubmate Doddie Weir had also made himself unavailable. When Scott Murray sustained a rib injury in the first Test and was ruled out for the remainder of the tour, the door was suddenly opened wide for second-row contenders to be capped. Iain Fullarton came on as the replacement for Murray in the Dunedin Test to partner the lofty Richard Metcalfe and held the position for the second meeting a week later. Fullarton, a Kelso player, who represented Scottish Schools while at Merchiston Castle in Edinburgh, was a surprise cap but a deserving one after impressive line-out displays in earlier matches.

New second row Iain Fullarton beats former All Black skipper Taine Randell to the ball during the first Test at Dunedin. Fullarton, winning his first cap, came on as replacement for Scott Murray, who incurred a rib injury.

If Fullarton had seemed an unlikely cap, then so did Nathan Hines, the replacement player in the tour party for the injured Scott Murray. The Australian-born Hines turned professional only in the summer of 1999, and missed most of the following season because of a shoulder injury. He more than any player took his chance. Played in the second half of the final midweek game against Hawke's Bay at Napier, Hines impressed sufficiently, with his sheer athleticism and ball skills, to win a place on the bench for the second Test. One to watch.

The Scotland tour was not all about new players coming forward. A number of experienced players reappeared on the international stage, among them Cammy Murray, the Edinburgh Reivers wing. Murray hit top form in the World Cup with a courageous display against New Zealand in the quarter-finals, his outrageous dummy to Jonah Lomu resulting in a try for Scotland. Then a shoulder injury killed his hopes of carrying his World Cup form through to the inaugural Six Nations Championship. In the event, Murray regained full fitness only a couple of weeks before the start of the tour, but by the second Test, and with a confirmatory display against Hawke's Bay, the Edinburgh Reiver was judged ready to make his Test comeback.

The other player to return to the international stage was the former Melrose centre Graham Shiel, who carried his fine late-season form with Edinburgh Reivers into the tour. Shiel showed his renewed appetite for the game with a skilful display against New Zealand Maori at New Plymouth, in a match the Scots should at least have drawn. There was no reward of a Test cap a week later, however, and instead Shiel had to be content with a place on the bench. For the final Test, however, the coaches had convinced themselves that Shiel was the player for inside centre, his selection marking a recognition of the need for a neat and skilful player at No. 12. 'Graham is now playing the best rugby of his career. But I've always said that the more genuine rugby players you have on the field, the more confidence there is on the ball and the more flexibility you have,' said McGeechan, shortly after the second Test.

The tour was not just about the development of players. Alan Tait, the former Rugby Union and Rugby League international back, was brought on tour as a defence coach to try to improve an area in which the Scots had been weak during the Six Nations Championship.

In terms of the results, outwith the Tests Scotland's tourists had mixed fortunes. The worst scoreline was the 42-16 defeat by a strong NZ Vikings side in the opening match at Whangarei. Scotland, anticipating an easier start to the tour, were cruelly exposed at the breakdown points and by their weakness in midfield defence, allowing the Vikings, containing future stars such as Tony Monaghan and Justin Wilson, to run in six tries.

The poor showing by Scotland brought an honest reaction from Bill Woodward, the Vikings coach. He said, 'Scotland must improve hugely in the contact area, otherwise they will be blown away. They're going to have a hard tour if they keep missing tackles like they did against us. At one stage in the second half we seemed to break tackles at will.' The warning was heeded. Against the combined East Coast/Poverty Bay side in Gisborne, Scotland shored up their defence and complemented this with a high strike rate, which included three tries from the Harlequins centre David Officer, to win 51-10.

The match against New Zealand Maori in New Plymouth was always going to be an early test of Scotland's readiness to face the All Blacks. The Maori side were defending an unbeaten record stretching back over 23 games. It was, de facto, a third Test match for the Scots. In the event, Scotland, playing some inspired rugby, came desperately close to winning, a missed penalty kick by Duncan Hodge allowing the New Zealand Maori back into the game to snatch victory with a late goal by full back Adrian Cashmore.

Scotland's fourth game – against Nelson Bays – was made more interesting by the presence in the Nelson squad of Craig Smith, the Melrose and Scotland U21 prop. Smith, in Nelson to improve his rugby, played the final quarter against his fellow countrymen and in the process staked a claim for higher honours. The 25-25 draw against the 1999 NPC second division champions was disappointing for the tourists but a reminder of the high standards throughout New Zealand rugby.

The remaining provincial match was against Hawke's Bay at Napier. Morale was low after the record defeat in the first Test at Dunedin. This was a

Craig Joiner glides past All Black centre Alama Ieremia in the second Test at Auckland. Although well beaten again, Scotland significantly reduced the margin of the defeat suffered in the first international. Coach Ian McGeechan was satisfied that much had been gained from the tour in developmental terms.

match the Scots had to win to regain the respect of the public. In the event, the tourists overcame the difficult wet conditions at McLean Park to post a 24-7 victory. 'It was very important that we performed well and showed the New Zealand public that we had the right attitude,' said McGeechan, adding, 'It was an immense performance to put in during the last week of the tour.'

The Hawke's Bay result undoubtedly put the Scots into a more competitive frame of mind for the second Test. At Carisbrook, the Scots had been torn apart by a rampant All Black side that ran in 11 tries, three of these by their world-class wing Tana Umaga. It was a record defeat for Scotland against New Zealand and one from which it was going to be very difficult to recover. In the event, McGeechan and his two assistant coaches, John Rutherford and Hugh Campbell, managed to motivate their side for a final effort.

Scotland made five changes to their side, one less than New Zealand, who were still experimenting with different permutations from their large pool. A New Zealand win was inevitable, but Scotland at least gained some satisfaction from reducing the margin of defeat and scoring tries through Cammy Murray and Chris Paterson. More importantly Scotland appeared to have absorbed the lessons of defence, but even the improvement in this area could not stop New Zealand's star players from showing their outstanding skills with a number of long-range tries.

No matter what they achieve in terms of tactical and technical skills, Scotland, it seems, will never produce players with the running abilities of the likes of Christian Cullen, Tana Umaga and Pita Alatini. Nor can they hope to compete with the likes of New Zealand with such a small base of players. These may be unpalatable truths for the Scots, for whom the hopes of ever beating the big southern hemisphere nations must now rest on the fact that rugby has a habit of producing the occasional upset.

HEINZ MEANZ TRIEZ

A GREAT SUPPORTER OF WORLD RUGBY

IRELAND IN THE AMERICAS

BY SEAN DIFFLEY

Ireland's season, following the poor showing the World Cup, seemed to have ground to a halt in the new century and the new Six Nations. The opening foray at Twickenham against England produced the most humiliating reverse of all time. It wasn't just the defeat – the Irish are fairly used to that at Twickenham – nor the awful margin of defeat that caused such upset but the total absence of traditional Irish resolve and fire. The players were heavily criticised, and the New Zealander Warren Gatland looked as if his days as coach of Ireland were about to come to an end. Shades of Lens in the World Cup, where the Irish were treated as such objects of scorn by the spectators, predominantly French, whose booing of a poor Irish side turned to derisive laughter before the final whistle against the deservedly popular Argentinians.

It was, indeed, the nadir as the Irish public and the media perceived it. That Ireland should recover so well was amazing. The oracle was worked through bolstering the side with a judicious infusion of some hardened Munster determination and the belated discovery that there was quite an amount of fine skill and speed among a roster of youngsters in the backs.

There was young Brian O'Driscoll in the centre, who was to romp over for three tries in Paris, where the French lost at home to Ireland for the first time in 28 years. That he could do so was due to the catalyst inside in young Peter Stringer at scrum half, whose quick wrists gave his outsides those vital fractions to react positively. Suddenly and quite unexpectedly Irish rugby had turned around. There was that Munster contribution in the pack from Keith Wood, Mick Galwey, Peter Clohessy and rangy Malcolm O'Kelly plus the new discovery at flank forward, Simon Easterby of Llanelli, whose mother was born and reared a hundred metres from the Blackrock College club.

And suddenly Warren Gatland was again the golden-headed boy and the plaudits rang, too, on his assistant, the backs coach, Eddie O'Sullivan, whose previous chores included coaching the American Eagles. Once again it was time to stop and smell the roses, and the grass was greener, too.

And then the epilogue. An end-of-season tour to Argentina, the USA and Canada. No doubt when the original decision to make the tour was made it sounded a good idea. It

Ireland coach Warren Gatland (right) and backs coach Eddie O'Sullivan on tour in the Americas. After a good finish to the Six Nations, their charges seemed tired.

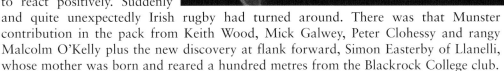

Ireland back-row forward Anthony Foley lines up Argentina's Gonzalo Quesada in Buenos Aires. The Pumas overcame the tourists 34-23.

most certainly did not turn out so. A bunch of very tired players made the trip with obvious lack of enthusiasm. Some managed to avoid the chore. Peter Clohessy, for instance, travelled, but his presence was due more to official diplomatic persuasion than to any personal interest in the project. Bits of blarney forced full back Dominic Crotty to tour and postpone his honeymoon. Brian O'Driscoll and Denis Hickie couldn't make it because of injury.

The net result? Another defeat by Argentina, in Buenos Aires, by 34-23. Ireland, playing their expansive game, were the better side in the earlier stages but ran out of gas before the end. Argentina outscored the Irish 23-8 in the last half-hour of the contest, which really tells its own story. Irish fitness levels, concentration and mental approach have so improved in recent times that it was obvious that already, in this first match of the tour, the season's pressures had produced such fatigue that it was all a bridge too far.

But the Irish were keen to stress that this was a good Argentinian team, and Pichot, the excellent scrum half, as he demonstrated in the World Cup, proved a great captain and leader for the winners. Losing to Argentina was no great shame, but the Irish could and should have won through impressive back movements, but tiredness intervened, and as one newspaper headline put it, 'Ireland miss killer instinct'.

Then it was on to Boston and the Test against the USA at New Hampshire. This one really brought to mind the old wartime question in the days of petrol rationing: 'Was your journey really necessary?' The Irish beat the USA by 83 points to 3, scoring a record 13 tries in the process against poor opposition. The American front five just collapsed, and the Irish owned possession and acted as would be expected.

As against Argentina, the Irish concentrated on the wide game, and the backs scored nine of the 13 tries. Geordan Murphy, the young Leicester player, too often thrown into wing duty, was impressive at full back, and the consensus was that he has put down a serious challenge for the berth next season. And Guy Easterby, Simon's scrum half brother, signalled, with his ability to make telling breaks, that Peter Stringer has a real challenger.

And so north to Toronto to take on Canada, who had just returned from a creditable performance in South Africa. Ireland were the only Six Nations side that Canada had never beaten, and it came perilously close for the Irish in Toronto on 17 June. It took a very late penalty goal from the ice-cool Ronan O'Gara to draw the game 27-27. The Canadians were the hungrier, more aggressive side. The Irish tried to continue the wide game that had been the motif in the end period of the Six Nations and in Buenos Aires

Geordan Murphy is brought to a halt against the USA. The result of the game was an easy victory for the tourists. Nevertheless, the Leicester utility back had an impressive game at full back and may have launched a serious challenge for the berth.

and New Hampshire, but nothing would go right for them in Canada. Simple passes were spilled and the Munster players in particular were very tired long before the end. If the 13 tries against the USA was an Irish record for a Test – beating the ten against Romania in 1986 and against Georgia in 1998 – the turnovers in this Toronto match against Canada must have constituted some sort of record, too. The Irish were lucky to escape.

Tours have been the lifeblood of rugby, but in these professional days, with the huge physical and mental demands on players, the obvious dangers of too much football and inadequate rest times must raise questions. Just a few weeks after returning home, the Irish tourists were back to the training grindstone again. Hopefully, they will have well recovered in time for the new season and to bring the policy of open, expansive rugby to new and successful heights.

BTcellnet

Football365
Planet-Rugby
Golf World

SURF THE BT CELLNE

SPORTS NEWS TO YOUR MOBILE

With BT Cellnet's new Internet phone you can access the latest sports results, fixtures and new from your mobile. So switch to BT Cellnet and visit some of the most popular Internet sites an access e-mails on the move. www.btcellnet.net

Connection to BT Cellnet is subject to status. Terms and conditions ap

THE HOME FRONT

TIGERS' REPRISE:
Leicester 1999-2000

BY **DAVID HANDS**

The fizz starts to flow as Leicester celebrate back-to-back Premiership titles after beating Bath at Welford Road in their final league match of the 1999-2000 season.

To help the end of the 1999-2000 season go with even more of a swing, Leicester chose the start of a new millennium to invite their supporters (of whom there are many) to select their best Tigers of the old century. There is a great temptation not to look much beyond the players who, in 1999 and again in 2000, brought the Allied Dunbar Premiership pennant to Welford Road, making their club the first in the professional era to win back-to-back championships.

Of course, the optimum XV, to be announced at the start of the 2000-01 season, will include players from other eras, but, whichever time they come from, they will be hard pressed to rival the collective spirit which animated Leicester throughout the longest domestic season the game has known. Dean Richards, who has led a charmed existence as Leicester's team manager, went on record at a very early stage to suggest that retaining the championship would be beyond his team. Richards, in his own quirky way, is a dab hand at motivation – some would suggest it is the inner strength which was so apparent when he played No. 8 for Leicester and England – but he knew only too well the effect the World Cup would have on his leading players. Leicester contributed 11 players to the

World Cup squads of England, Scotland, Canada and South Africa, and it was not so much their absence during October that nearly scuttled their Premiership prospects as their form when at last they returned. It is impossible to forecast how the most talented of individuals will play when they stand down from the adrenalin rush that is the World Cup; those who have played only a limited role for their country are anxious to release all that pent-up energy, while those who have appeared in every game only to see their efforts end in failure are lost in a mist of anticlimax.

Leicester's low point coincided, however, with the Heineken Cup, which followed hard on the heels of the World Cup. Their European campaign faltered from the start, but it had only a limited impact on their Premiership form, which had been so well sustained by a new generation of Tigers. If one match persuaded the Welford Road hierarchy that all was not lost, it was the home game against Bristol in October, when their teenaged half backs, Andy Goode and James Grindal, showed their skill and appetite for the fray, and Pat Howard's experienced head drove his young colleagues on.

If it was a remarkable season for Leicester, it was no less so for Howard. The 26-year-old Australian played in every Premiership game and concluded by agreeing to stay a further year as player-coach with responsibility for the backs, in succession to Joel Stransky. His consistency, his willingness to accept responsibility and physical punishment in order to establish a platform for the club's powerful forwards were key ingredients in keeping the Leicester show on the road and in the translation of Austin Healey from international wing to fly half.

Leicester's young scrum half James Grindal kicks from the base of the scrum against Wasps at Welford Road.

It was a brave, possibly desperate, decision. Healey joined the club in 1996 to play scrum half, the position in which he won his first England cap and toured with the British Lions in 1997. England converted him back to the wing, where he had played for Waterloo, but to give him the pivotal role at a time when the club fortunes were ailing was an act of faith triumphantly vindicated by subsequent results. Healey had three persuasive arguments in his favour: his own footballing abilities and astute brain; the advice of Stransky, whose exploits in the No. 10 jersey for South Africa included the dropped goal that won the 1995 World Cup final; and the presence at his side of Howard, who has played fly half himself at international level and understood the stresses and strains of the position. It could be argued that Healey's success in the role contributed significantly to England's capture of the Six Nations Championship and

NEXT

Official Clothing Sponsors Leicester Tigers

led directly to his appearance – admittedly in a dire emergency and with only 90 minutes' warning – at fly half for England against South Africa in Pretoria in June.

Yet few would have forecast a Premiership title in a season which linked Healey and Jamie Hamilton at half back and saw Martin Johnson appear in no more than ten of the 22 matches. Johnson, England's captain, was struck down by an Achilles tendon injury in mid-season and his return was delayed after concussion received during a training collision with Craig Joiner. Since Joiner is eight inches shorter and four stone lighter than Johnson, the club jesters had ample material for their wit, although Johnson possibly did not see the funny side.

Thus it was that, as late as February, Northampton and Gloucester surveyed the rest from the top of the first division, with Bath fast coming up on the rails after a mid-season glitch. There were those who backed Northampton to take an unprecedented treble, so well were they performing, although Leicester might have advised caution on that front – in 1997 they had been in the same position as their midland rivals and ended up glad to win the Tetley's Bitter Cup. Indeed, the fact that they could concentrate solely on the Premiership enhanced Leicester's charge as the season worked its way into its fourth quarter. Northampton, with Heineken and Tetley's balls in the air, found they could not operate successfully on three fronts, and Gloucester discovered their squad did not have the strength in depth to sustain a challenge.

That Leicester took up the gauntlet from Northampton was a source of some delight: on the opening day of the Premiership season, the Tigers crashed 46-24 at Franklin's Gardens and then received a mauling from Gloucester at Kingsholm, which left them lurking among the bottom four in the division. But the young bloods – Ben Kay at lock, Will Johnson in the back row, Leon Lloyd at centre – took up the cudgels with such determination that they gave their seniors a fighting chance when they returned from the

Tim Stimpson prepares to put his trusty right boot to effect in the home game against Bristol in October 1999. Stimpson scored 321 Premiership points and was selected for the England touring party to South Africa in the summer of 2000.

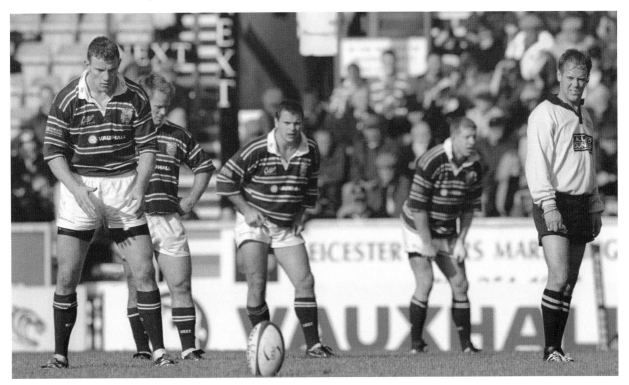

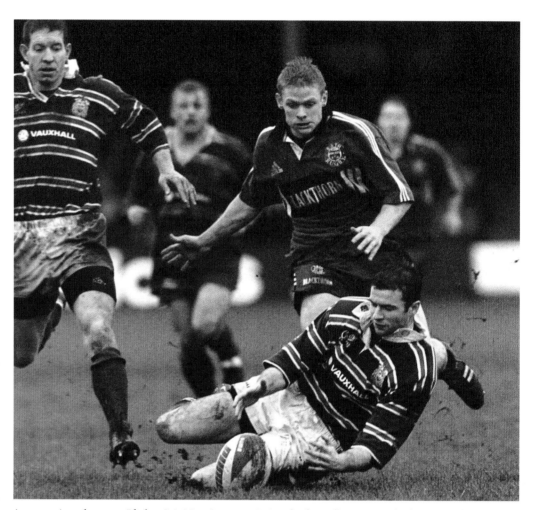

Leicester's Geordan Murphy reaches the ball ahead of Bath's Iain Balshaw at the Rec in the Boxing Day 1999 league clash that the Tigers won 13-3.

international wars. If the 36-19 win over Bristol, then flirting with the top of the table themselves, was one turning point, so too was the one-point win at London Irish a week earlier. There was the confidence of players willing to express themselves allied to the consistent boot of Tim Stimpson, which provided a buffer against disappointment in so many games. Stimpson, disappointed to be omitted from England's squad, registered 321 points in the Premiership and virtually forced his way back into the England touring party to South Africa during the summer.

The first phase of the Premiership ended in mid-November, with Leicester handily placed in third position behind Bath and Gloucester. Their travails during the Heineken Cup were reflected in the tousing by Saracens at Vicarage Road, but they discovered the ideal antidote: success at Bath, where they had fought so many memorable duels during the amateur era. It was a dank Boxing Day made bright for Leicester by their 13-3 win, the only try coming from another player of growing influence, Geordan Murphy. Like Healey, Murphy is blessed with handling skills which allow him to play full back, wing and fly half with almost equal facility, and he scored nine tries in 19 Premiership appearances en route to a first Ireland cap on tour in the Americas during June.

By the time the Six Nations Championship arrived in February, Leicester had conquered their mid-season blues. That they contributed Healey, Darren Garforth, Neil

Back and Martin Corry to England did not prove a problem, since that quartet returned bubbling from England's successes (until the unexpected hiccup against Scotland on the final weekend of the championship). Leicester were able to ride out the dip in form of so talented a centre as Will Greenwood and uncovered a little diamond at prop in Ricky Nebbett, once of Harlequins but whose contribution during the final weeks of the Premiership was outstanding.

Leicester hit the top with a somewhat 'iffy' win at Bedford in March, and although Bath overtook them, they did so only because they had played two more games. Yet it was apparent that if anyone was to deny Leicester it would be their old friends from the West Country. As the season neared its climax, Leicester moved two points clear of Bath with a game in hand and, as luck would have it, found themselves in a position to clinch the verdict at Bristol. A host of neutrals hoped for a Bristol win so that, on the season's final day, Leicester and Bath would slug it out at Welford Road. It was not a scenario Leicester favoured, so Murphy, Lloyd and another rapidly improving youngster, Lewis Moody, scored the tries that ensured a 30-23 victory over Bristol. Thus the Tigers could parade the trophy in front of their own faithful a week later and add a double over Bath by way of a grace note. That they are champions with a primarily England-qualified side, with more on the way, is an example that others might follow; that they have an unheralded but effective coach in John Wells is a throwback to the amateur days; significantly, there is more to come from a young playing squad and a young management team.

ENGLAND'S MISSING INGREDIENT

BY EDDIE BUTLER

Twickenham, HQ of rugby's Establishment. But are the England team on the brink of throwing off the shackles of conservatism and joining the world ranks?

It is not often that English rugby finds itself at the cutting edge of confusion. In the long, chaotic history of a complicated game, England had always stood for conservatism. Twickenham was the Establishment; change was only a dirty collection of coins one kept to put in one's godson's piggy bank.

Faced with a revolt at the end of one century, which led to the breakaway by the northern clubs and the birth of Rugby League, Twickenham could not have played the part of aristocratic overlord better. Money was filth; the working classes that wanted broken-time payments were worse. Threatened by revolution exactly one hundred years later, Twickenham's traditional defence crumpled beneath the mantra of market forces. In 1995 amateurism was no longer a principle but hypocrisy. Like the rest of the rugby-playing world, England turned professional.

And ever since then, the railway they built in the days when the chaps knew a thing or two about engineering and timetables has been a bucking, white-knuckle ride through the Wild West. Club owners, broadcasters, militants from the grass roots and middle-of-the-road managers have all tried to service or derail the train in equal measure.

The most emphatic reason why England have not been able to dominate the world of rugby in the past couple of seasons is that, instead of operating in an environment of order and harmony, there has always been a riot going on in the background. It's like the Fat Controller trying to show off his railway to a potential purchaser by highlighting such attractions as a calm area for the elderly, only to find Thomas the Tank Engine and Gordon the Express having a stand-up shunt in the marshalling yard.

A country that fails to embrace the conditions of the new age cannot expect to be dominant. Other countries that took to professionalism, that had paved the way, were obviously going to have an advantage. As the southern hemisphere giants moved seamlessly into the Tri-Nations Series, England tried to impose a moratorium. When they found this head-in-sand approach was not going to work they signed a television deal with BSkyB that took the Five Nations to the very brink of disintegration. Then came the wage hyperinflation started by Sir John Hall at Newcastle, followed by the flood of overseas players, which left the England coach with all of two home-qualified outside halves to select from in the top division.

Given this state of chaos – which could yet be reactivated at any moment, despite the best efforts of the Rob Andrew Report to put the train back on track – it might be considered remarkable that Clive Woodward has managed to make England a credible force at all, let alone a major player on the world stage. That may excuse England for losing to New Zealand and South Africa in the 1999 World Cup. It does not explain why they lost to Wales at Wembley and failed to win the Five Nations Grand Slam one year, and promptly repeated the mistake the next by failing to beat hapless Scotland at Murrayfield and missing out on the first Grand Slam of the Six Nations.

England may have floundered in the early years of the paid era, but so have the other European countries. France dominated at first because they already had an infrastructure in place to run their semi-professional game and were better able to handle the new demands of open remuneration. But France now have political and commercial squabbles that put England in luxury coach F on the Orient Express.

And what about closer to home? In Wales and Ireland it took years to recover from the shock of being dropped stone cold into commercial sport. Scotland may have won the last Five Nations of the second millennium but their yo-yo international form and the icy relations between the Superdistricts and the feeder clubs suggest that they are still traumatised by the sea change of five years ago.

Whatever the outrage around the shires of England – which manifested itself in the peasants' revolt that placed the crown briefly on the head of Cliff Brittle at Twickenham – and whatever the monies poured down the clubs' wage-drain, Woodward in the past three years has been given all the support he asked for to build Club England at the centre. He has more technical back-up than a starship, more medical know-how than the sickbay of the *Enterprise* and more

Coach Clive Woodward at England's training camp at The Couran Cove Resort, Australia, in June 1999. In the past three years Twickenham have been willing to provide Woodward with all he has asked for in order to build Club England.

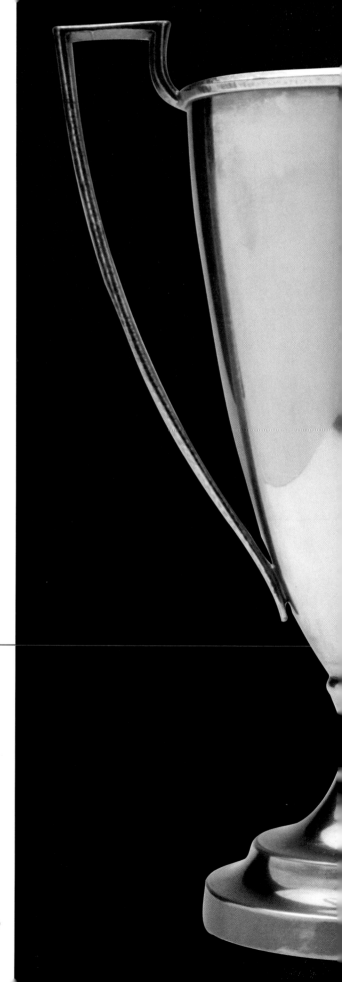

A top team in the field of law.
One step ahead of the game.

winning

Wragge&Co

55 Colmore Row Birmingham B3 2AS England
Telephone +44(0)121 233 1000 Fax +44(0)121 214 1099
e-mail: mail@wragge.com   website: www.wragge.com

expert analytical input than the space between Mr Spock's ears. And still he loses to the Welsh and Scots.

But that's the way it has always been. England have always had countless more players to choose from than the rest of their neighbours put together. And not just more of them, but bigger too. In the old days, England had taller, broader and more powerful forwards than everyone else. The counterbalance was that they never used their backs, who were faster than everyone else's, and never took the game as seriously as, say, the Welsh, for whom rugby was – is – an expression of defiance against an unloved neighbour.

Woodward's demands for ever better facilities, and Twickenham's preparedness to invest in them, are a sign that England are now taking this game seriously, too. England players are still bigger than most and certainly fitter, the difference most markedly apparent when they took Wales apart at Twickenham in the first Six Nations.

And they have changed their game, not just to be able to dominate Europe but to give themselves a chance of putting together the six games in succession that will make them champions of the world. They have lost only twice in the last two European championships – as above, to Wales and Scotland – and in general have given everyone else a right old lesson in the ways of the modern game.

But this is a nation that for over a century was the very essence of conservative thinking. The need for change may now be intellectually embraced, but deep down the Englishman instinctively veers towards the traditional, particularly at times of stress. Even the Italians in their first season in the big time knew how to press the buttons that

'England players are still bigger than most and certainly fitter…' Lawrence Dallaglio carries half of Wales over their goal line to score in the Six Nations encounter at Twickenham, which England won 46-12.

Like the Grand Slam, the missing ingredient remained 'out of reach, out of range'. Contrasting reactions greet the final whistle at Murrayfield, as Scotland beat England to deprive them of a Slam, just as Wales did a year earlier.

would make England lose their multi-faceted cool and revert to the predictable and starched. England could not possibly lose to Italy, but they did lose to Scotland. The missing ingredient remained just that: something out of reach, out of range. And then they went on tour to South Africa, and the English revolution truly began. Slowly at first, because in the first Test in Pretoria there were still signs that they could be dragged down to a game played in blinkers. But in the second Test in Bloemfontein they played with an energy and a breadth of vision that could be the start of something spectacular.

So, what is the missing ingredient? What is the difference between England at soggy Murrayfield, where they should have won but lost, and Bloemfontein on the High Veld, where history suggested they had to lose, but where a majestic reality asserted itself? Is it Clive Woodward himself? His sideways elevation to the post of manager might suggest that he has recognised some failing in himself and considered it time for Andy Robinson to take over. Is Woodward's propensity for communication by e-mail or in real language that is sometimes hard to decipher to be replaced by the blunter delivery of the former back-row forward with whom Woodward worked at Bath?

It cannot be about the message or delivery now. Vision was always more important than language, and on that front Woodward was spot-on all along. The great question was: could England ever take the leap and stay flexible and adaptable under pressure? They could train in as many exotic locations as they liked, and add as much variety as they could, from the Gold Coast off Queensland to Lympstone with the Marines, but could they play when the great squeeze was being applied by the top teams?

You can rehearse as many penalty kicks as you like, but only the loneliness of being out there in front of 75,000, with the posts 45 metres away and the scoreboard telling you that this is the last chance, will tell you if you are up to it. Similarly can you make the right decision to offload before the tackle, or make yourself available for the pass when all you want to do is have a whiff? Just two more breaths here at the bottom of this ruck and then I'll be on my way. It's so easy just to stay half a yard back and the ball won't come my way, and nobody will ever know. This has nothing to do with coaching now. Nor with committee-room investors, or back-up scientists, or car park attendants at Twickenham. It has everything to do with the minds of the players and their confidence. With how to undo all the years of conservatism and play with a simultaneous relaxation and passion.

To shape the body and attitudes of the professional rugby player sounds pretty easy, time and money being no problem. And Clive Woodward took England a very long way into a new world. But the final, missing ingredient is the most elusive. The only way to conquer lack of breath and lack of space is to frequent rugby at its most intense as often as possible. But there you run the risk of encountering the physical exhaustion that can ruin everything. And there you find yourself up against opponents who are all doing exactly the same thing: searching for the elixir that will transport them to the top of the pile. To beat the Wallabies, the All Blacks want to control the footie better, the Springboks want additional pace in phase play. And on it goes. England's ambitions coincide with those of the other top nations. The only difference is that England, since the start of this journey through an increasingly complex sport, have never been number one in the world. Their rugby history is telling them not to bother, but in the heartland of the Free State of South Africa they may have discovered a state of freedom that allows them at last to contemplate not just winning every prize in the game but in a manner that electrifies the game and secures the future prosperity of rugby.

The difference from that April day at Murrayfield when the Grand Slam dream melted could hardly be more marked. In late June, England celebrate beating South Africa at Bloemfontein to tie the series. Have they discovered the missing ingredient?

GRAHAM HENRY: THE BEST MAN FOR THE JOB?

BY **PAUL ACKFORD**

On the inside or on the outside? Can Graham Henry, here at a Wales training session in 1998, get the respect of the Lions and guide them to victory over Australia?

Graham Henry's appointment as coach to the 2001 British Lions has split rugby opinion right down the middle. On the one hand there are the 'British is best' diehards who cannot stand the fact that a New Zealander will be in charge of the most talented group of rugby players Britain and Ireland have to offer as they attempt to put one over on the Wallabies. How can a Kiwi even begin to understand the tradition and culture of the Lions? they ask. How will he have any credibility when he stands up in the dressing room 15 minutes before the final Test with the series tied at one all and asks them to lay their bodies on the line for Queen and country or whatever. Roger Uttley, the great ex-England and ex-Lions player and coach, was so vexed by these questions that he wrote to the letters pages of the *Daily Telegraph*, criticising the Lions selection committee for going with Henry and ignoring British candidates.

But then there is the other viewpoint, which is best summarised as 'to hell with the bloke's nationality, the only question worth asking is "Is he the best man for the job?"'

And here Henry's CV is pretty impressive. An 80 per cent success rate with the New Zealand province Auckland and, in the early days at least, an equally decent track record with Wales. Henry added spine and detail to the Welsh effort, guiding them to wins over South Africa, England and France. This guy knows what he is on about, say the Henry fan club, and in the professional era with multiple migration of players, coaches and ancillary staff, it doesn't matter a jot where a fellow hails from.

Gareth Thomas tries to evade Cobus Visagie (No. 3) and Werner Swanepoel during Wales' 29-19 victory over South Africa at the Millennium Stadium in June 1999. This was just one in a line of Welsh successes presided over by Graham Henry.

As for me, I'm with the pro-Henry mob. I played for the Lions under Scotland coach Ian McGeechan at a time when the rivalry between England and Scotland was unhealthily hostile and never once did nationality become an issue. Being part of the Lions is all about submerging differences, about coming together under one banner, and the origins of the coach, just like the origins of the players, will not matter one bit.

Respect is the key to coaching – respect for the values of the individual, his rugby knowledge, his commitment to the common cause, his judgment, his reaction to the disappointments which inevitably accompany any major tour, his communication skills. If Henry can get a handle on most of those areas, then he and his Lions are in for a good time. With a bit of luck, they may emulate their 1997 predecessors in South Africa and defeat the champions of the world, which is precisely what Australia are at the moment.

There is no identikit answer to what makes a good coach. In the late 1980s, before England organised themselves into a worthwhile national outfit, the Rugby Football

Union paid for a scouting mission Down Under to see how the southern hemisphere boys did it. The RFU wallahs made no bones about it. They were out to copy best practice and introduce it back home.

The stuff which filtered back was mind-boggling. The RFU spies found that some of the training sessions of one of the better known provinces took place in a glorified cowshed and involved a series of rucking and mauling drills in which players were bounced off the roughened concrete walls of the building as they went in search of the ball, while the coach bellowed encouragement like an enraged bull. Legend has it that in the bath afterwards some of the players sported road rash grazes on elbows and shoulders which would have made a boy racer envious.

Now, you and I might think that those training methods were unnecessarily cruel or brutal or both, but the point is that neither the players nor the coach saw anything wrong in that session. It was just the way they did things in New Zealand years ago. It wouldn't have worked in England of course. That kind of attitude was missing back then, but New Zealanders did not complain, because they had been involved in those sessions since the Dead Sea was sick, and another one wasn't going to make any difference.

McGeechan, the best coach in British rugby over the past decade, would have had a dicky fit if someone had told him to run a session like that. Not because Geech was soft. Far from it. Some of his training sessions had players begging for a breather halfway through. No, Geech was more cerebral in his approach. His practices were designed to empower the players, to give them the confidence to play the game as they saw fit rather than slavishly follow a pattern. The Lions blossomed under McGeechan in 1989 and 1997 because there were men on both of those tours who welcomed the responsibility

Sealed with a kick. Jeremy Guscott takes the responsibility and drops the goal that finished off South Africa in the second Test at Durban in 1997. That Test victory brought Ian McGeechan his second series victory as Lions coach.

thrust upon them. It didn't make Geech a better coach than the New Zealander in the cowshed. It was simply a different way of doing things and, in any case, the only justification of a coach's philosophy and methods is the scoreboard at the end of a game or a tour. Win, and training in points and a tutu was a good idea. Lose, and it's back to the drawing board.

There are only two lessons worth learning for any coach. The first is that he must be himself. Players can spot a fraud straightaway, whether it's someone talking tosh about something and not admitting it, or someone who plainly has not updated himself in the practices and theories which drive modern rugby. The game is littered with instances where great players ten years ago have been appointed as coaches only for them to discover that the sport has moved on and what sufficed when they were playing is now hopelessly old-fashioned and irrelevant.

The only other lesson worth taking on board is that the coach must do his own thing. It was a mistake for the RFU to think that they could transpose what worked in New Zealand back into the English environment. The cultural differences were too great for starters. It was also crass to try to play catch-up, because you can bet your shirt that in the two or so years it would have taken English rugby to understand and assimilate what the New Zealanders were trying to do, those pesky All Blacks would have moved on and redefined the objectives.

Clive Woodward understands that lesson. When Woodward took over England from Jack Rowell, he made it perfectly clear that he would attempt to take England forward in a way which suited the players, the finances and the political set-up. He moulded his ideas and ambitions around what he thought was peculiar to English rugby as a concept and what would work on the global stage.

Opposition in waiting – the world champion Wallabies. 'There is nothing more appealing to a New Zealander than stuffing it up an Aussie team, especially when they are the only nation to have won two World Cups.'

Woodward took the national squad down to the Royal Marines training base outside Exeter; he insisted on top-notch, personalised treatment for his men, including named cubicles in the Twickenham changing rooms; he communicated with his players through e-mails which came through on their private laptops; and he generally tried to create a culture of excellence. In the early days there was much mirth as Woodward unveiled his latest madcap scheme, but of late there has been general agreement that he has raised the standards of the national squad, developed an outstanding crop of young players and invested in the future. For the first time in living memory England are close to narrowing, perhaps even closing, the gap which has traditionally separated the two hemispheres. There was no blueprint for Woodward to follow. He simply trusted his instincts and applied the principles he valued from a successful business career.

Therein lies the challenge for Henry. He has just about been long enough in Wales now to understand the context in which rugby operates in Britain and Ireland. He knows, too, a lot about the various strengths and weaknesses of his potential Lions touring party through his association with the Five – then Six – Nations Championship. And there is no question whatsoever that he will be totally versed in what Australia are likely to come up with. There is nothing more appealing to a New Zealander than stuffing it up an Aussie team, especially when they are the only nation to have won two World Cups.

The only concern with Henry is that he might fail to appreciate the importance of the Lions. He will know they are box office from his time in New Zealand, but he won't understand it from the inside. When Henry first arrived in Wales, he took time to appreciate the particular intensity and rivalries which apply to the Six Nations tournament. He admitted that the whole thing took him by surprise, quite caught him out, in fact. He will not have that luxury with the Lions. If Henry does not get it right from the start, by the time he has settled down, the tour will probably have gone down the pan – which is why it was such a shrewd move for the Lions selection committee to team up assistant coach Andy Robinson and manager Donal Lenihan with Henry. Both those guys are British rugby veterans through and through. Both are ex-Lions themselves and both are not afraid to pull Henry aside and tell him his fortune if they think that the tour is heading ever so slightly off the rails.

So give Henry a chance all you doubting Thomases. Allow him the luxury of selecting a touring party and playing a few matches in Australia before you write him off. True, he is not British. True, he has not even been over here for much more than an extended holiday. But he is a coach of genuine stature, he has performed minor miracles with an underpowered Welsh team, and he is, by a considerable distance, the best man for the job.

REACH FOR THE BEST

It's rare to find a recruitment consultancy who tackle personnel requirements with such tenacity and unfailing dedication. An unrivalled approach that has enabled Pertemps to remain unchallenged at the top of the league as the UK's leading independent recruitment consultancy.

As market leaders, we have developed our reputation not just by "filling positions" but by adding value to our client portfolio, a philosophy which is reflected in the diverse range of leading blue-chip companies that currently utilise our services.

Operating in three service divisions: commercial and professional, industrial and driving and technical and executive, our fully integrated service ensures that we are able to deliver quality personnel with the right skills, in the right place at the right time.

So, if you are seeking to win the competition for business, make sure that you retain the competition for talent by choosing Pertemps, Britain's most successful independent recruitment consultancy.

PERTEMPS
recruitment partnership

HEAD OFFICE:
Meriden Hall, Main Road, Meriden,
Warwickshire CV7 7PT.
Tel: 01676 525000 Fax: 01676 525009
Email: info@pertemps.co.uk
Web Site: www.pertemps.co.uk

Cannon Centre

At insp@ce we have
developed a unique approach
to real partnering with our clients.
As a service provider, we deliver
creative, innovative and comprehensive
interior and fit-out solutions.

Our reward is your complete satisfaction.

Fortnum & Mason

insp@ce

INTERIORS AND SPACE SOLUTIONS

Dedicated to providing solution

insp@ce would like to wish the best
of luck and our continued support
to the Wooden Spoon Society
Rugby World '01.

Nikko Bank plc

Hilton Hotels

TETLEY'S BITTER CUP: grand final or grand finale?

BY **ALASTAIR HIGNELL**

'If it ain't broke, don't fix it.' The players in the Tetley's Bitter Cup final delivered the message in emphatic fashion; 55,000 fans at Twickenham had to agree; and the game's mandarins, contemplating a playing structure that could find no room for the cup, were forced to question the wisdom of binning one of their proven assets.

The 29th National Knockout Cup final was fit to rank alongside any of its predecessors. Passion, commitment and the resultant unforced errors are to be expected in any showpiece final; so too is the ecstasy of the winners and the agony of the losers. This one also had tension, as the lead changed hands an unbelievable eight times; controversy, as three players were sent to the sin-bin; and a grandstand finish, with both sides having chances to win the match in the closing minutes. That Wasps should prevail showed as much about their state of mind – this was their third successive final – as about that of a Northampton side whose treble-chasing season seemed suddenly to be in danger of disintegration. The fact that, for the first time, the winners would automatically qualify for Europe added immeasurably to both the tension and the lustre of the competition. So too did the decision to stage the semi-finals back to back at the neutral venue of the Madejski Stadium in Reading. To both the uncommitted and the partisans at Twickenham it seemed doubly ironic that just as the cup was getting its act together the game's governing body seemed determined to close it down.

One argument against its retention is that, unlike its soccer counterpart, it produces few real surprises, and that as the game at the top end becomes more and more professional the chances of an upset decrease while the chances of serious injury to a mismatched player increase. That argument suggests that Northampton's 118-3 fourth round win

over Nuneaton does nobody any good. Few, though, would deny the likes of Darlington Mowden Park their moment of glory – in the same round they beat Rosslyn Park, three divisions above them – or their day in the sun: their reward was a fifth round trip to Harlequins. And none surely would quibble with London Welsh's preference for an Old Deer Park quarter-final against Northampton, even if the alternative was a guaranteed £35,000 to forfeit home advantage. The cup at least gives junior sides the chance of rubbing shoulders with the big boys, even if the chances of defeating them are getting slimmer by the year. With the leagues becoming increasingly ring-fenced, many feel it could be the only chance they get.

In between their predictable victories over Nuneaton and London Welsh, Northampton had to survive the fiercest of fifth round examinations by Saracens at Vicarage Road, the Saints going through by the skin of their teeth and the proverbial coat of paint as an injury-time match-winning dropped goal from Saracens outside half Matthew Leek was controversially ruled to have gone wide. Following their Old Deer Park triumph, Northampton had to subdue London Irish – the form team, with home wins in previous rounds over Leicester and Gloucester – in the Reading semi-final.

Wasps, meanwhile, had been granted a bye in the fourth round, as holders; suffered a scare in a fifth round repeat of the previous year's final against Newcastle; and thrashed Manchester 62-3 in the quarter-finals. They were in imperious form, too, for the first hour at the Madejski, posting 44 points without reply against Bristol, before surviving a late onslaught from the West Countrymen, who ran in five tries and 31 points of their own.

Come the final, Wasps were undoubtedly in better form, better shape and a better frame of mind. True, Northampton had beaten them in the Heineken Cup quarter-finals with a late and controversial Paul Grayson penalty, but nothing could shake their sense of injustice or their belief that they had been the better side. They had just avenged a home league defeat by the Saints in the autumn with a 50-point victory at Franklin's Gardens in a fixture which, it was decreed, had to be played just four days before the Twickenham encounter. They had the unlooked-for motivation provided by remarks attributed to Northampton owner Keith Barwell that Wasps had 'some iffy players' and that his side were '20-30 points the better', and they had all their players fit, relaxed and focused on what all but mathematically was their last chance of qualifying for Europe.

Northampton, by contrast, were in pieces. That midweek defeat by Wasps was their fourth in a row in the league. It also meant that for the first time all season they were outside the top four automatic European qualifying places. They had, it's true, qualified for the Heineken Cup final, but another last-gasp win – over Llanelli, also at the Madejski – had taken its toll on the nerves, and the bodies. Club captain Pat Lam and England captain Matt Dawson had both been forced from the field at Reading with serious-looking injuries. The Northampton list of walking wounded was growing.

Shane Roiser tries to give Ben Cohen and Budge Pountney the slip, as his skipper, Lawrence Dallaglio, monitors events.

It was no surprise, therefore, that Wasps started the better. A series of attacks led to a simple opening penalty for Alex King. It was no surprise either that after the ever-reliable Grayson had levelled and then snatched the lead for the Saints, Wasps should reassert control and post the scores that, at half-time, pointed to only one winner.

First, full back Josh Lewsey powered over on the left after good approach work from his forwards. Then, after two Grayson penalties and one from King, Wasps hooker Trevor Leota barged his way over from close range on the right, and King knocked over another penalty to establish a 19-12 lead at half-time.

At that point, it seemed easy to gloss over the fact that the Wasps outside half was having a shocking afternoon with the boot, landing only three from six, because his team seemed well in control. Lawrence Dallaglio, Paul Volley and Joe Worsley were winning the battle of the back rows; locks Andy Reed and Simon Shaw were always in the thick

*Let the party begin!
Four times runners-up
in the cup before their
triumph last season,
Wasps now refused to
let the trophy go.*

Centre Mark Denney celebrates his injury-time try as members of the Wasps contingent, including England hooker Phil Greening, queue up to congratulate him.

of the action; and the front row of Will Green, Leota and Darren Molloy were holding their own against more vaunted opponents. By contrast, Northampton's heavier, older forwards seemed spent. On a baking-hot afternoon it seemed they would wilt still further. Behind the scrum, Dawson and Grayson seemed unusually hesitant, Allan Bateman was uncharacteristically subdued and the back three of Ben Cohen, Craig Moir and Nick Beal never looked like escaping Wasps' defensive blanket. Wasps, crucially, had survived a seven-minute spell when they were down to 13 men. A flurry of yellow cards from referee Brian Campsall had seen centre Rob Henderson and flanker Paul Volley despatched to the sin-bin, as well as Northampton hooker Fred Mendez, all within three minutes of each other. While thus reduced, Wasps even managed to score through Leota. The match was theirs for the taking.

But while Wasps relaxed at the start of the second half, Northampton, as they had done so often in the season, dug deep. As Leota missed his jumpers at a line out and King missed a penalty that would have put his team more than a score ahead, Grayson kicked his fifth penalty and Budge Pountney burrowed over for a try from a line-out take by Richard Metcalfe. Grayson added a record sixth penalty and suddenly, with 14 minutes left and completely against the overall run of play, the Saints were 23-19 ahead.

The final whistle couldn't come quickly enough for Northampton's exhausted players – and it didn't. Wasps outside centre Mark Denney, on the day completely eclipsing opposite number Allan Bateman, first found a gap, then found Lawrence Dallaglio in support. The former England captain's brilliant pass out of the tackle allowed Kenny Logan an unopposed run to the try line. Even then Wasps weren't home and dry. Paul Grayson had won two Heineken Cup ties with last-gasp penalties from long range. From 52 metres, with two minutes to go, he had the chance to make history again. His kick fell short, but Leota made such a hash of dealing with it that the Saints had one last chance to attack. Moir, it appeared, had the line at his mercy, only for flanker Joe Worsley to wrap him up in a try-saving, match-saving tackle. Denney then confirmed that it was to be Wasps' afternoon with an injury-time touchdown.

Wasps – with the exception of Lewsey, who was due back at Sandhurst to resume his first week of officer training – could embark on the mother of all parties, safe in the knowledge that they'd booked their place in Europe next season. Northampton could set off up the M1 to lick their wounds in the knowledge that they would be back at Twickenham a fortnight later for the final of the Heineken Cup. The crowd of 55,000 fans could head for home in the knowledge that they had witnessed a great rugby spectacle. Only the powers that be would know whether it was the last of its kind.

MY LIONS TO AUSTRALIA

BY **MICK CLEARY**

Jeremy Davidson secures line-out ball for the Lions in the first Test against South Africa in Cape Town in 1997. Ireland's Davidson is included in our squad to Australia in 2001. His second-row partner, Martin Johnson (at the right of the picture), is also in, once again as captain.

Endless fun, endless argument, endless futility. No matter how long we thrash out the issue; no matter how considered our opinion, how huge our ego – we'll never get the exact make-up of a Lions party right. And the reason is simple. It is not our own ineptitude (albeit a significant factor) nor the amount of Theakston's Old Peculier that might have addled the thought processes. No, the answer is altogether more elusive than that. It is to do with form, with the endless and changing patterns of a season that sees one player in great shape in September and performing like a one-legged goat in late May. Injury and fatigue also play their part, as does that great selector in the sky who toys with us all as we try to counter the ravages of age.

Just take the last Lions tour to South Africa in 1997 as an example. Who would have chosen Paul Wallace and Tom Smith to anchor the front row? Or Jeremy Davidson to pack down alongside tour captain Martin Johnson in the second row? Alan Tait and John Bentley – where did these names suddenly spring from? They were all worthy contenders but a long, long way from being front-runners. The English pack, in particular, had been the dominant force for many a day, and most observers (this one included) expected the men in white to be the backbone of the forwards.

And now? Who might we pick as Lions scrum half, for example, for next summer's trip to Australia? Lob in a few names. Matt Dawson and Kyran Bracken from England, Ireland's slick, graceful Peter Stringer, or the robust, rejuvenated Andy Nicol of Scotland. But what about Wales? I hear you ask. Who was their main man at the end of the Six

**A FULL BACK
WITH PLENTY OF CLASS.**

Nations Championship? Good old Rupert Moon, of course, a fine son of Llanelli and a wonderful ambassador for the sport. Now, Rupert Moon wouldn't pick Rupert Moon for the Lions squad, much as his open, refreshing, upbeat character would be a boon to any touring party. No, Moon himself admitted when he got the unexpected call-up from Graham Henry after five years in the wilderness that he wasn't the most polished of scrum halves.

There is no doubting who was, and still is – Rob Howley. Howley, though, has had a nightmare year. He lost the Welsh captaincy, lost his place and, finally, lost his cool, falling out with one Graham Henry. And yet Howley was one of the real gems of the 1997 Lions party. As he sat poolside at Umlangha Rocks, just outside Durban, one Sunday morning, arm in sling, face down round his ankles, most of us were revising our predictions for the first Test the following week. Howley had smashed his shoulder to pieces the previous day against Natal and was on his way home that night. Howley, smooth, smart, confident, was the linchpin of the Lions. He set the tempo; he called the shots. Out he went, in came Matt Dawson, and six days later we all rose to salute one of the great tries in the history of the game, as Dawson sold an outrageous dummy, foxing half the South African population in the process, to help nudge the Lions into the history books. A week is truly a long, long time in sport.

But Howley would be one of the men I would write down now, for form is temporary and class is permanent. The real doubt is not Howley's ability but his relationship with Henry. Can those bridges be mended? Who will make the first move? Delicate stuff. If the rift is too deep to heal, then Stringer should get the nod. Who is this bloke? And who is that alongside, in the red of Munster and the emerald green of Ireland? His schoolmate and fellow-traveller Ronan O'Gara, the coltish, ruddy-cheeked Corkman, is another to have taken the unexpected limelight this past season. They were unknown outside their

Although not first choice for Wales at the end of the 2000 Six Nations, Rob Howley is a class act and a must-have Down Under. Here he launches an attack against England in the 2000 clash at Twickenham. In support is Colin Charvis, another inclusion in our Lions squad.

province at the start of the Six Nations Championship; by the end, with Ireland winning in Paris for the first time in almost 30 years, they were the talk of every rugby town.

Henry was a controversial choice as Lions coach. Ian McGeechan was the first option, but the three times Lions coach decided that he was not able to juggle his commitments to Scotland with those of the Lions. McGeechan is conscientious to a fault. Only he knows, though, just how much goes into setting up a successful Lions tour. He is quite convinced in his own mind that the most important work for the victorious 1997 trip was done 12 months earlier.

'I spent a good deal of time that summer in South Africa,' says McGeechan. 'New Zealand were on tour and beat the Springboks for the first time ever on their soil. It was quite a series. I saw at first hand just what sort of game we needed to play in order to beat South Africa. I drew up a list there and then of the players I thought would fit the pattern. It was also a great advantage to have several lengthy chats with the All Black management throughout the trip, coach John Hart and captain Sean Fitzpatrick. The fine detail, of taking an enlarged squad to give the back-up specialist players at scrum half and hooker a midweek rest, the scrum machines, medical staff, was crucial.'

And that is why Geech reluctantly turned down the offer this time around. He did it his way in 1997 and didn't feel it possible to devote enough time to the cause this time around. Henry will, and should, do it his own way. There is no doubting his raw coaching abilities. He has been involved at the highest level for many years. There are all manner of doubts, though, about his background. Henry is a New Zealander – a simple statement with many overtones. For all those who have backed his corner, the Lions committee for a rather big start, there are an equal number who object, and object strongly, to a foreigner in the camp.

Feelings are running high. Roger Uttley, John Jeffrey and Clive Woodward are three former Lions to have had their say against. The Hastings brothers were also uneasy over the appointment. Ah, you might say, all former players, all men perhaps living in the past. What do the current players feel about the arrangement? Why haven't we heard their views on the subject? Easy. Listen to this off-the-record remark from one leading player. 'What do I think of Graham Henry being Lions coach?' he asked. 'Surprised, to say the least. But to get me to say that on the record is a non-starter. The key thing about the Lions is getting selected in the first place. I'm not daft enough to jeopardise that situation.'

Fair enough. But Henry is smart enough to know that he will have to win over a few doubters within his own playing party. He will also have to tune in to the fact that he has only a desperately short time to bring his men together, to somehow create an immediate mood of togetherness and trust that everyone instantly buys into. McGeechan, along with Jim Telfer and Fran Cotton, were immensely successful at doing just that in 1997. Henry has to do so again. And for that to happen he has to select well.

He needs men who have the respect of their peers – for their playing ability first and foremost and for their commitment to the Lions cause as well. All nationalistic grudges have to be buried instantly. Let's start with the captain. England alone have three contenders – Matt Dawson, Martin Johnson and Lawrence Dallaglio. Three good men and true, all Lions, all perfectly capable of doing the job and doing it well. Ireland can offer up that great Lion Keith Wood. I'd go for Johnson. He was a huge hit in 1997, and on England's summer tour to South Africa showed that he is in tip-top condition.

Props? A long list. Smith again from Scotland, so too Wallace from Ireland. Peter Clohessy, also from Ireland, is too old, warrior that he is. England can offer Jason

Leonard, Graham Rowntree, Phil Vickery, Julian White, David Flatman, while Wales weigh in with the form props, Dai Young and Peter Rogers. Five to travel for me: Rogers, Young, Flatman, Vickery and Smith. Three hookers would give us Keith Wood of Ireland, and Phil Greening and Mark Regan from England. The locks should be Johnson, Bath's Steve Borthwick, whose star will rise this season, Scott Murray, Chris Wyatt and Davidson.

The back row is tricky – fiendishly tricky. Look at the runners and riders: Dallaglio, Richard Hill, Neil Back, Joe Worsley and Martin Corry from England alone. Budge Pountney steamed through last season for Northampton and Scotland, while Colin Charvis and Scott Quinnell have very respectable credentials. Big Scott could be the one to miss out.

Fly halves? Not exactly packed to the rafters. Jonny Wilkinson is in pole position, while one of the '97 stars, Gregor Townsend, can also fill a slot. Has Neil Jenkins has his day? O'Gara is showing strongly but has some way to go yet to prove that he can survive under fierce scrutiny.

The centres throw up all sorts of fascinating combinations: the new Irish wonder boy, Brian O'Driscoll, with Scotland's John Leslie. Has Allan Bateman, so resilient, so crafty, so classy, got enough left in the tank? Will Scott Gibbs hit the heights again? And Will Greenwood? Mike

Right: England's outstanding back row of Back, Hill and Dallaglio, seen here celebrating victory over South Africa at Bloemfontein, are elected en bloc in our tour party.
Below: Ireland's Brian O'Driscoll skips around Stephane Glas on his way to three tries in Paris in 2000. Could he form half of a series-winning combination in the centre?

Tindall is developing alongside Mike Catt, who has had his best year of international rugby. Wales' Mark Taylor is another to watch. My six would be O'Driscoll, Tindall, Catt, Gibbs, Leslie and Greenwood.

Wings – a real choice. England's Iain Balshaw is a truly exciting prospect, while Dan Luger is a proven finisher. Ben Cohen had a tremendous Six Nations, and Austin Healey has shown that he can worry the best defences. Kevin Maggs is more a centre than a wing so could provide cover. Finally, full back. Step forward Matt Perry of England, Rhys Williams of Wales, Glenn Metcalfe of Scotland.

There you have it, for now at any rate, a 39-man Lions squad to beat Australia. The three extra men will be needed in this era of endless replacements. Believe me, the script will change weekly.

The squad: M. Johnson (England, capt); M. Perry (England), R. Williams (Wales), G. Metcalfe (Scotland); I. Balshaw (England), A. Healey (England), D. Luger (England), K. Maggs (Ireland), W. Greenwood (England), S. Gibbs (Wales), B. O'Driscoll (Ireland), M. Tindall (England), M. Catt (England), J. Leslie, (Scotland); G. Townsend (Scotland), J. Wilkinson (England), R. O'Gara (Ireland), R. Howley (Wales), K. Bracken (England), M. Dawson (England); P. Rogers (Wales), D. Young (Wales), D. Flatman (England), P. Vickery (England), T. Smith (Scotland), K. Wood (Ireland), P. Greening (England), M. Regan (England), S. Murray (Scotland), J. Davidson (Ireland), S. Borthwick (England), C. Wyatt (Wales), L. Dallaglio (England), R. Hill (England), N. Back (England), J. Worsley (England), M. Corry (England), B. Pountney (Scotland), C. Charvis (Wales).

Mike Catt is also in our squad, as is Ireland's Kevin Maggs, on the end of this Catt pass. A third potential Lion in shot is Bath second-row Steve Borthwick (to Maggs' right).

CHELMSFORD MINI FESTIVAL

BY PETER JORDAN

Former Leicester and England fly half Les Cusworth puts the minis through their paces. Looking on is Chelmsford's Brian Garbutt.

At the start of the 1974-75 season, Chelmsford Rugby Club decided to create a mini-rugby section, a fashionable thing to do at the time. The 'minis' proved to be very popular, so much so that three Chelmsford stalwarts, Tony Steene, Alistair Graham and Colin Ash, proposed that at the end of the season the club should organise a mini-rugby festival as a high point of the first mini season. No sooner was it proposed, than the dynamic threesome were given the go-ahead to proceed, and so was born what is believed to be the oldest continuously held annual mini-rugby festival in England.

The first festival attracted a collection of those clubs within Essex and East Anglia who had taken up the game of mini rugby and was something of a mix of funfair and family day with mini rugby thrown in. However, Chelmsford very quickly learned from their first experience, and the second festival, at the end of the 1975-76 season, featured more mini rugby and less funfair. This festival really gave the first inkling of how popular mini rugby was becoming. More than one thousand people turned up, and the number of clubs wishing to attend also increased dramatically, creating something of a headache for the organisers. However, everyone was accommodated, even though this meant the playing time stretched to five hours from the original idea of four.

There was no question now but that the festival had become an annual event, with teams attending from the South Coast and even from as far away as Wales. This popularity had its own drawbacks, however, in that the organisation began to creak with the sheer number of teams and spectators attending. On the plus side, this popularity

Former Scotland and British Lions full back and captain Gavin Hastings says a few words. Alongside him on the dais is festival organiser Colin Ash (left) and Chelmsford club president Bob Gammie.

meant that Chelmsford were able to attract personalities from the world of rugby to attend and to present the trophies and certificates to the players and coaches. Among these celebrities were Gavin Hastings, Rob Lozowski, Peter Winterbottom, Roger Uttley, Kyran Bracken, Jason Leonard, Paul and Richard Wallace and, last but by no means least, Ian Robertson, who, in fact, has appeared twice in support of the event. Many of those who have attended the festival will remember the inspirational words of Gavin Hastings, Roger Uttley and particularly Ian Robertson.

Roger Uttley was especially good, considering that the Chelmsford club arranged for him to be collected from an England coaching session somewhere in the West Country and delivered to Chelmsford by helicopter, courtesy of a club member's friend who owned a helicopter charter company. Nobody at Chelmsford was aware that Roger suffers quite badly from motion sickness, as was witnessed by many British Lions players on a calm boat trip to the Great Barrier Reef. Roger did not enjoy the flight, needless to say. However, he recovered very rapidly to spend hours mingling with the crowd and to give a first-class speech at the awards ceremony, despite the fact that he was to be helicoptered back to Harrow School after the event. To all those who have honoured the festival in this way, without recompense, the Chelmsford club extend their sincere thanks.

Unfortunately, with the advent of professionalism in Rugby Union it has become much more difficult to obtain the patronage of international standard players, unless clubs are prepared to pay substantial fees. This seems a great pity as mini and junior rugby are the lifeblood and the future of the game and deserve the full support of the senior clubs.

During the 25 years of the Chelmsford Festival there have been some amusing incidents, mainly interactions between referees and spectators, and also players and spectators. Several of these episodes have involved Mrs Thatcher's favourite weapon, a well-loaded handbag, wielded by an irate mother. To be fair, these incidents have been few and far between, with the vast majority of coaches, spectators and players ensuring that the aim of the festival – to encourage fair play and total enjoyment for the children – is fully achieved.

About ten years ago it became obvious that mini festivals can become similar to 'Topsy', in that they can grow and grow to the point where they become unmanageable. The then Chairman of Youth and Mini Rugby, Tony Hoult, together with his team of mini managers, decided to draw up a blueprint for the ultimate in efficient festivals. This involved inviting only a limited number of clubs who were able to provide teams throughout the age groups, and ensuring that there were a substantial number of referees together with a fully staffed control to co-ordinate results. So successful has this blueprint become that is has been adopted by Eastern Counties as an ideal of future mini festivals.

Throughout the whole 25 years, one man has made a lasting impression on all the festivals. That is Colin Ash, one of the event's founders. He has manned the microphone through rain and shine (thankfully mainly shine) and has entertained us all with his ready wit and his enthusiasm for the sport.

A lasting reminder and a real bonus for the club is the fact that several of the players who took part in the very first festival are still playing for the senior club. More recently three of the club's former minis have progressed to play for Northampton U19, with one player, Mike Rosen, representing England in the U18 Four Nations Tournament held in Ireland during April 2000.

The enthusiasm for the festival is as strong as ever, and during the last few years, under the control of Mini Manager Mike Barnett together with Mini Secretary Kay Jones, the festival has evolved into a very efficient and superbly organised event. Long may it continue.

The Chelmsford RFC U11 side with former England and British Lions flanker Peter Winterbottom. How many of these youngsters will still be playing for Chelmsford in 25 years time?

ROTHMANS R.I.P.

BY STEPHEN JONES

For the first time in almost 30 autumns there will be no *Rothmans Rugby Yearbook* this year. Last year's was the 28th, and barring some sort of Lazarus-like revival next year, possibly under a new sponsor, then that is that. It is a sad end for what Bill McLaren always called 'my rugby bible', and even though a 28-year sponsorship, such as that of Rothmans, is not to be sniffed at in terms of commitment, nothing goes on for ever. No doubt *Rothmans*' loyal core readership will be very disappointed that the familiar dark blue book will not be on their shelf.

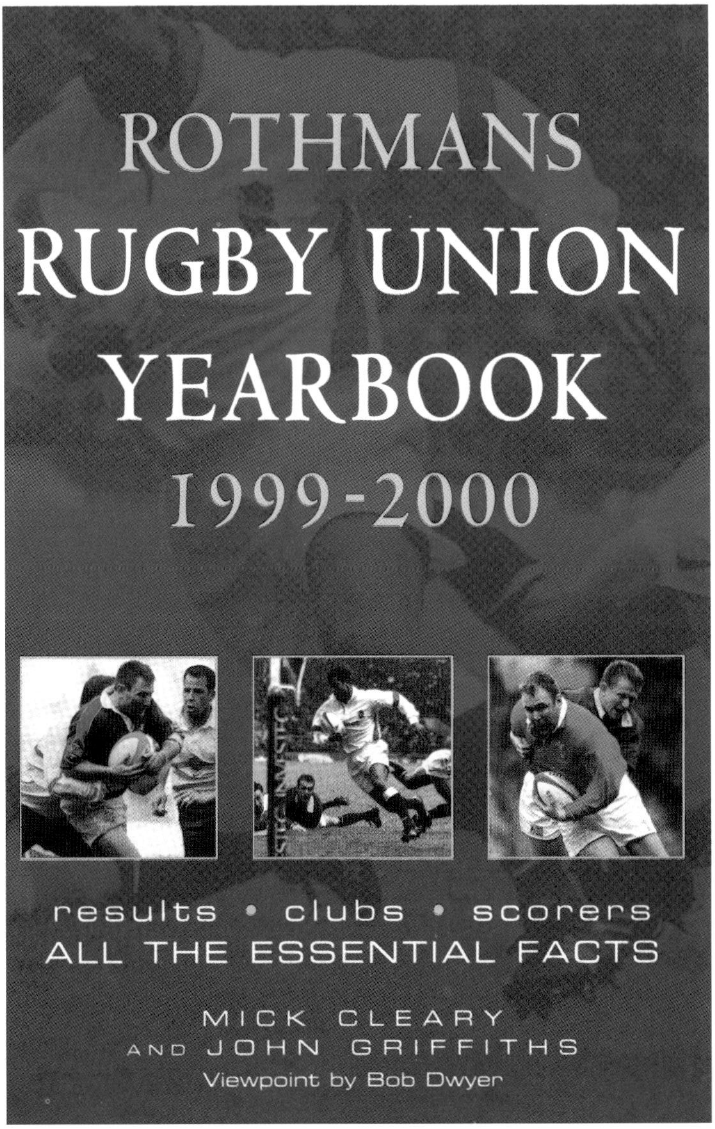

The yearbook was started after it absorbed the *Playfair Rugby Annual*, making its first appearance in 1972. It began under the editorship of Vivian Jenkins, the great former Wales full back and *Sunday Times* rugby correspondent – then in retirement – and it was the zeal, enthusiasm and professionalism of that great character which gave life to the whole thing. Jenkins was meticulous and industrious and carried on as editor for ten years.

At some point in that time he had ensnared me – whoops, I mean called me up – for menial tasks, while he assessed my suitability for taking charge of the world's leading rugby statistical record. Amazingly, despite all the evidence at his disposal, he appointed me to succeed him in 1983. It may be quite an admission, but I am conceivably rugby's

Right: The 28th and final edition of Rothmans Rugby Yearbook *in the now-familiar dark blue covers. Opposite, top right: Vivian Jenkins, former Wales full back,* Sunday Times *rugby correspondent and first editor of the yearbook. 'It was the zeal, enthusiasm and professionalism of that great character which gave life to the whole thing.' Opposite, below right: The author, Stephen Jones of the* Sunday Times, *'conceivably rugby's least dedicated statistician', who took over from Jenkins in 1983.*

ROTHMANS
RUGBY UNION
YEARBOOK
1999-2000

results • clubs • scorers
ALL THE ESSENTIAL FACTS

MICK CLEARY
AND JOHN GRIFFITHS
Viewpoint by Bob Dwyer

least dedicated statistician – a bit like someone appearing on an advertisement for drinks and then admitting that he is teetotal. To supervise such a book is not a pleasant or a fun task, it is hard graft. Staggeringly, I managed to hold out against my better judgment and was also editor of *Rothmans* for ten years.

Any guilt I felt about not being a statistical genius was then forgotten as I handed over to Mick Cleary – a man with so little grasp of stats that he has been known to miscount the number of children he has, and for that he has only to add up to four. Cleary took over in 1995 and saw home the next five editions up to and including the 1999-2000 edition, the last. Three editors in 28 years is not much of a turnover. There were also major contributions from Queen Anne Press and Headline, who published all 28 editions between them. For almost all of that time, the house editor was Caroline North.

Rothmans Rugby Yearbook 1972

Editorial Advisor: **VIVIAN JENKINS**
Compiler: **IAIN MACKENZIE**

£1·50

Right: It wasn't always blue. The first edition of the yearbook, published in 1972. Opposite, top right: Mick Cleary, Rothmans *editor from 1995 to the final whistle, pictured before being exposed to the 'hard graft' of supervising the yearbook. Opposite, below right: Caroline North, 'a brilliant house editor and one of rugby's unsung heroes'.*

I may be biased because she also acts as my literary agent (sounds grand), but Caroline was a brilliant house editor. She would be uncomplaining every year as Cleary or myself disappeared to the southern hemisphere in spring and left the whole operation in near shambles. One of rugby's unsung heroes.

Of course, all this talk of non-statistical genius might make you wonder where on earth all those brilliant statistics came from – all the tiny details of caps, matches, records, tours. You might also wonder how they managed to be so brilliantly accurate, because it was extremely infrequent that any of the millions of statistics were proved wrong. Many people – from their garrets or from their notebooks or even from international rugby unions – wrote in to query this or that statistic, some of them in haughty mode. I can hardly remember a single occasion when our statistics were proved wrong, even down to the middle name of someone who played in the 19th century. So talk about unsung heroes and you have to talk about John Griffiths, the book's statistician and, lately, joint-editor.

It was Viv Jenkins' finest legacy that he discovered Griffiths, a Welsh-born and Watford-based schoolteacher. Griffiths was to update and transform rugby's records, and to this day he still does. I am not aware of anyone in the rugby world, anyone working in journalism or any media or any union, who does not regard John Griffiths as the premier statistician and record-keeper in the history of the sport. People have tried to test him and he is never found wanting. I would trust John's work with my last penny. Any self-respecting publication or website would be well advised to sign a deal with Griffiths rather quickly.

It is, of course, the websites which have partly cooked *Rothmans*' goose because websites can be updated daily, or at least after every significant match. Not everyone has access; not everyone wants access. There will still be thousands of people who would rather have a book on their shelves than have to gain access via a computer, but the often fragile business structure of a book can be upset by just a small percentage drop in readership. It was also obvious that in its current format *Rothmans* was totally inadequate – the old eight top countries are now besieged by so many others, and there are so many more big matches. The only alternative was to produce a book of around twice the current size, but then the economics would all be out of kilter again. Shame. It has been part of rugby, part of our lives. It reflected a game that was keen on statistics, if not obsessed by them, as are American sports. Especially through Jenkins and Griffiths, it provided a good service to rugby. Maybe one day it will reappear in bigger and better form, and the first job then will be to sign up the redoubtable Griffiths.

He tells one of the best stories of *Rothmans*' dedicated readers, even though it is against himself. An Australian reader wrote in the late 1980s to say that he thought that details of three Australian caps were missing. He had added up the total number of individual caps awarded to Australian players in the book. Then he added all the matches his country had ever played, multiplied by 15, added on replacements, and found, so he said, that three caps were missing. Griffiths sent back a nice letter and almost forgot about the query for five years. After that five-year gap, the same Australian wrote in again. He had found that A. Morton had won three caps against New Zealand in 1958 and they were not recorded. It was true, and is likely to be a mistake of typesetting rather than of Griffiths. For the 1995-96 yearbook, the caps were restored and all was well.

SAFE HANDS

www.cheltglos.co.uk

Cheltenham & Gloucester
Looking after your best interests

C&G MORTGAGES

For a range of attractive mortgages and investment accounts, backed by a track record for value and outstanding service, just get in touch with Cheltenham & Gloucester.

For more details contact us on:

0800 454 305

Fax: 01452 373681

REVIEW OF
THE SEASON
1999-2000

Our Lloyds TSB
Live! rugby programme
reaches 150,000
11-16 year olds each year.

SCHOOL

Lloyds TSB

THE LLOYDS TSB SIX NATIONS CHAMPIONSHIP

BY ALASTAIR HIGNELL

Try telling Clive Woodward that lightning never strikes twice. For the second year in a row, his England team went into the last game of the season with a Grand Slam and a Triple Crown at their mercy. For the second year running, they ended up with neither. This time they also surrendered the Calcutta Cup. At least they had already done enough to become the first ever winners of the Six Nations Championship.

For this was the year that Italy joined the party. The omens were not good. The team that had come within a whisker of beating England in a Rugby World Cup qualifier 18 months before had, judging by some dismal results in the finals, gone past its sell-by date. The players who had inspired the *azzurri* to recent victories over Ireland, France and Scotland were growing old together and the coach Massimo Mascioletti had been replaced. Worse was to come when inspirational captain Massimo Giovanelli suffered a serious eye injury and had to retire from the sport altogether.

But not before the dynamic flanker had led his team to a stunning opening-day victory against the reigning champions, Scotland. Ian McGeechan's men were ambushed in Rome's tiny Stadio Flaminio stadium by the highly motivated Italians, superbly prepared by new coach Brad Johnstone and brilliantly directed by veteran outside half Diego Dominguez. Dominguez kicked three dropped goals in a record 29-point haul. Italy's victory, by 34 points to 20, was thoroughly deserved. So were the front-page headlines in a soccer-obsessed country. For rugby to take root, the Italians need many more results like it.

They weren't to get them in the year 2000. Their three away matches, in Cardiff, Dublin and Paris, delivered some sobering home truths, and their return to Rome saw them waste a spirited start against England. In all five matches the Italians conceded 228 points. But they scored over a hundred themselves, and although they lost Giovanelli at

Paris belongs to me. Brian O'Driscoll is paraded around the Stade Français after scoring three tries in Ireland's 27-25 victory over France.

What a start! Championship debutants Italy have just beaten Scotland 34-20 in the Stadio Flaminio, Rome, with fly half Diego Dominguez (left) scoring 29 of his side's points. To his right is Massimo Giovanelli, who was soon forced to retire from the game with a serious eye injury.

the beginning of the campaign and Dominguez, through retirement, at the end, that victory against Scotland and the emergence of talented youngsters like flanker Mauro Bergamasco and props Andrea Lo Cicero and Tino Paoletti ensured that their first championship season ended in credit.

France went the opposite way to their European neighbours. They, too, began the season with a new coach, Bernard Laporte succeeding Jean Claude Skrela, but whereas the Italians had disappointed in the World Cup, the French, in reaching the final, had exceeded all expectations. By the start of the Six Nations in February, something was missing. So were a large number of key players, through injury. Nevertheless France opened their Six Nations account in style, crushing Wales 36-3 in Cardiff. But for some heroic English defence in Paris, especially when down to 13 men in the closing minutes, and the inexplicable decision by captain Fabien Pelous to run a penalty rather than go for a set scrum, Laporte might have been contemplating winning the championship at the first time of asking. Instead, the injuries continued to pile up, and confidence, despite victory at Murrayfield, continued to ebb away. By the time Ireland came to Paris, to secure their first win in the French capital for over a quarter of a century, the Stade de France had become a 'bogey ground' for the home side. Victory over Italy in the final match of the campaign did at least end a sequence of five defeats at the Stade, but the win was as nervy and unconvincing as the team itself.

By contrast, Ireland's win in Paris had the men in green jerseys looking at a record undreamt of since their only Grand Slam of 1948. Victory in their final match against Wales at Lansdowne Road would give them four consecutive championship victories in a season and, moreover, would leave England needing to beat Scotland to claim the title outright. Humiliated by England in their opening match, the Irish had made wholesale changes for the visit of Scotland. They worked – in spectacular fashion – as Ireland overcame a 10-0 deficit to score five tries in a 44-20 victory. A fortnight later they ran six past the hapless Italians, while a hat-trick from brilliant young centre Brian O'Driscoll inspired an extraordinary comeback and that historic win over France. Defeat by Wales in Dublin was an anticlimactic end to the season for the Irish – two late Neil Jenkins penalties the ultimate difference between the two sides. But their consolation was the knowledge that in O'Driscoll and the half backs Ronan O'Gara and Peter Stringer they had unearthed some rare talents for the future.

Wales, too, could be proud of bringing on the youngsters. Wing Shane Williams made his debut in defeat against France, scored his first try in the win over Italy and ran in two more against Scotland. Outside half Stephen Jones scored 16 points on his full debut in that match and 12 more, including a try, against Ireland. Full back Rhys Williams showed outstanding promise when winning his first cap in Dublin. The Welsh season, however, was overshadowed by 'Grannygate'. Revelations that New Zealand-born full back Shane Howarth and flanker Brett Sinkinson had been playing without the necessary grandparental qualifications saw both players ejected from the team to play Scotland.

Wales full back Matt Cardey is suitably delighted as flying machine Shane Williams scores the first of his two tries against Scotland at the Millennium Stadium.

For the second year running, England could not pull off the Grand Slam, going down against the Auld Enemy in the rain at Murrayfield. Here Lawrence Dallaglio and Richard Hill try to bring Scotland's Martin Leslie to a standstill.

Ironically, their departure coincided with the return to Welsh colours of English-born Rupert Moon, long since qualified by residence. Victory in those last two matches was a testament to the character of the team. Crushing defeats by France and England earlier on in the campaign showed just how far the Welsh still had to go.

Scotland also had a disappointing Six Nations. That last-day win over England, the first for 11 years, was sweet enough, but neither coach Ian McGeechan nor stand-in captain Andy Nicol was hailing it as anything other than a one-off match when everything they had planned had gone right. They could complain that the luck had been against them from the start: caught cold by the Italians, they had lost their captain John Leslie for the season before the campaign was a few minutes old. They had run into Ireland on the rebound from humiliation by England and a Wales team desperate to draw attention away from 'Grannygate', and had been undone by two flashes of brilliance from French flanker Olivier Magne at Murrayfield. Victory over England at least prevented the 1999 champions from ending up with the first wooden spoon of the new millennium.

As for England, the Murrayfield defeat was a blow to the solar plexus. It was as if the previous year's experience – when a last-minute Scott Gibbs try had cost England the match against Wales and the Grand Slam – and the intervening World Cup campaign had taught them nothing. At Wembley they had shown tactical naivety in opting to kick for touch rather than at goal in the final few minutes. At the Stade de France in the quarter-final against South Africa, they had been suckered into playing a game of aerial ping-pong. Now, in the wind and rain of Murrayfield, they found themselves playing the way Scotland wanted them to and, frustratingly for their coach and their fans, they seemed incapable of changing their approach. On the day they didn't deserve to win.

They did, though, deserve the championship. Matt Dawson, the man most guilty of that last-day tactical inflexibility, had been an inspirational captain from the moment he was chosen to replace the injury-stricken Martin Johnson. His demonstrative and passionate leadership had encouraged those around him to express themselves in high-scoring wins over Ireland, Wales and Italy, and to man the barricades in Paris when France laid late siege to their line.

England, like Ireland and Wales, also brought on their young players: wing Ben Cohen and hooker Phil Greening had sensational first championship seasons, while centre Mike Tindall and his Bath colleague Iain Balshaw gave glimpses of great things to come. Of the more established players, in the backs Austin Healey was at his irrepressible best, Matt Perry confirmed his growing reputation as a world-class full back, while Mike Catt reinvented himself as an inside centre; in the pack the tried and trusted back row of Lawrence Dallaglio, Neil Back and Richard Hill continued to hit their own high standards, and Garath Archer and Simon Shaw made light of the absence of first-choice locks Martin Johnson and Danny Grewcock. If a Lions squad had been picked at the end of the season, most of the players would have been English.

They still may make up the bulk of the party to Australia at the end of the 2000-01 season. With three home matches – against Scotland, France and Italy – England must be favourites to defend their title. France, surely, won't be as troubled by injuries as they were in 2000 and should run them close. Bernard Laporte's men will be the benchmark against which Lions manager Donal Lenihan and coaches Graham Henry and Andy Robinson can measure the young hopefuls. If the coming season can bring forward as many exciting young players as the last, they can count their blessings. If it can produce as many exciting and unpredictable matches, so can the fans.

England skipper Matt Dawson charges away from Wales' Colin Charvis during England's emphatic 46-12 victory at Twickenham.

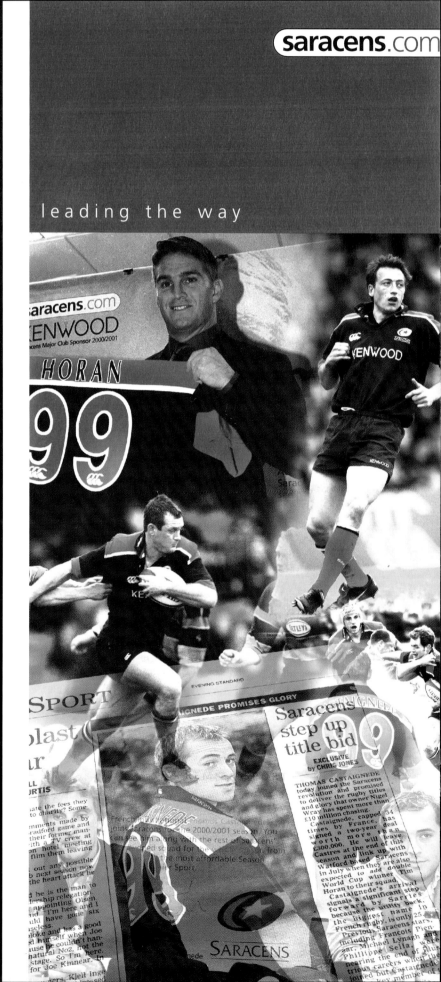

THE CLUB SCENE

ENGLAND – The pluses have it

BY BILL MITCHELL

Yet another season of professional rugby has passed by in England, and as usual there have been pluses and minuses, but at last the former outweigh the latter, which is encouraging. For a start, it would seem that in the new season there will be some consistency in the compilation of fixtures and there will be no movements of goalposts at the end of it, as has happened in each of the post-amateur seasons to date.

Commencing in 2001-02, there will be a new super league of (probably) a dozen English clubs, and these will be well subsidised by sponsors so that bankruptcies, which have virtually accounted for Richmond and London Scottish, should in theory be a thing of the past. But sponsors themselves need a square deal and if it is not forthcoming they can swiftly remove their much-needed help – and it does not need a genius to work out the subsequent problems. Until now, too many top clubs have spent money as if it had only just been invented and have then expected to be bailed out by the RFU, a situation that cannot go on.

Fortunately, however, a bright scheme suggested by some sugar daddies – the British League – is not in danger of being implemented. In theory, everyone would make millions from this idea, but as with other grandiose plans the danger would always have existed that, if huge attendances did not materialise, the wealthy sponsors would decamp, leaving clubs with huge debts and players on lucrative contracts having to find other employment, as has already happened with Richmond and London Scottish. There is a full season for the organisers of the new Premier League to work out the details in a satisfactory way. One of their ideas has – rightly – been knocked on the head. They wanted no promotion or relegation for at least two years, but this idea runs contrary to all concepts of fair play and common sense and is a non-starter.

There is also a big idea that franchises, baseball-style, should be established in certain cities, which

Robert Todd of London Irish is pulled down by Manchester Sale's Peter Anglesea. Irish are leaving the Stoop and moving to Reading. Will their supporters follow them?

would seem to be a recipe for problems, since the experiment of moving Richmond to Reading in 1998-99 proved that new supporters are not readily available – at least in the numbers that are needed for survival. The effective demise of both clubs seems to have been lost on London Irish. They have effectively been banished by Harlequins from a shared arrangement at the Stoop Memorial Ground, because they were enjoying better support than the host club, and seem to think that a move to Reading can work. One must wish them luck, because they will need it. For a start, they may find that loyal supporters have no enthusiasm for a drive along the M4 on Saturday afternoons.

The franchises idea presupposes that crowds will flock to see something new, but most franchises will occur in places where traditional rugby clubs with a basis of loyal support already exist, so would it not be better to build on those foundations? After all,

Northampton's inspirational Samoan captain Pat Lam is grabbed by Neath's Robbie Jones in this European Cup clash at Franklin's Gardens. Northampton went on to win the trophy, their sole success in a season that saw them in the hunt for a treble.

attendances have improved in recent seasons and good rugby will bring its own rewards, provided that too much is not expected of players and spectators. By this I mean that we probably have enough competitions with last season's return to Europe, so a planned British Cup or even a league cup would be asking too much.

However, enough of strictures! On the whole, in playing terms it was a good season in England, with the national team (Murrayfield apart) playing very well after a sad World Cup exit. The final month provided some excellent fare. The Tetley's Bitter Cup final at Twickenham was again won by Wasps (31-23), this time against Northampton, who had their chances and might well have won the match. They were only a single point adrift in injury time and with an inviting ruck in front of the Wasps posts to exploit. Instead of giving Paul Grayson a chance to drop a probably decisive goal, an attempt to run the ball for a try failed, and Wasps instead scored at the other end to retain the trophy.

Decisive action in the hour of need
Denotes the hero but does not succeed. (Belloc)

The Tetley's Bitter Cup is said to be scheduled for downgrading, with some super cup, involving only elite English clubs, or a British Cup taking over. The people who think that this is a good idea would do well to consult other sporting leaders for advice. After all, the FA Cup for the round ball game owes its glamour in many ways to the fact that smaller clubs are able to enter and that shocks from these minnows beating star sides are not unusual.

Northampton were compensated a couple of weeks after the Tetley's match with a narrow victory (9-8) at Twickenham over Munster in the European Cup final. This time the luck was with them on a wet afternoon when Grayson's boot was decisive and poor Ronan O'Gara for the Irish team missed all his chances at goal. We were all thankful to be spared the puerile entertainment which was served up at the Tetley's Bitter final. Is it necessary to greet every score with canned music over the public-address system? Or is it a good idea to humiliate some poor mortal by asking him to try to win a million by kicking three goals from easy positions and then watching him fail dismally? Would not a meaningful curtain-raiser have been a better plan? The County Cup final, for example?

The Allied Dunbar Premiership provided much excitement also, but it soon became clear that Leicester, whose cup season had been decisively ended by a thrashing at London Irish, would have ample compensation by gaining a comfortable win in the league. The standard of play in the competition was generally high. One feature – sad to some – was that the play-off for first division promotion and relegation was won by

Rotherham celebrate receiving the Premiership Two trophy after their match against Wakefield at the end of April. Rotherham secured promotion to Premiership One by seeing off Bedford in the play-offs.

Rotherham, who narrowly beat the unfortunate Bedford this time round. Thus Rotherham completed a full house of elevations after starting in the lower reaches of the Yorkshire leagues, which in itself provides a case for movements up and down. Bedford's demise may prove to be in their best interests, since they had a wretched season and won only one league match. Regrouping in Premiership Two may not be a bad thing for them.

Speaking of Premiership Two, both Leeds and Worcester gave Rotherham a good run for their money and will sooner rather than later be rewarded for enterprising management. Poor West Hartlepool finished bottom of the division and go down again. They are replaced by Otley from the first division of the Jewson National League, in which now-struggling Blackheath ended the season in last place with another poor record. Kendal (North) and the ambitious Esher (South) move up a notch from the two Jewson regional leagues.

In other spheres, there was encouragement in the fact that Oxford and Cambridge continue to atttract huge crowds. This latest Varsity occasion was a double-header – the U21 sides also played – and featured a brace of thrilling matches. For once in a while Oxford did the double over their traditional rivals, an outcome which came about despite the tactical genius of the Light Blues' guru, Tony Rodgers. His charges started off brilliantly against a good Dark Blue team. But Oxford had too much strength in the second half and overturned a 13-3 half-time deficit to win narrowly with a late try from Sherriff. As it happened, there was a larger attendance at this match that at the Tetley's Bitter final – a good vote of confidence for the amateur game.

The BUSA title was won by Northumbria, who triumphed over Loughborough in a low-scoring (14-8) match at Twickenham. However, the Midlanders' ladies made amends in part by beating Cardiff's UWIC 15-10 in their final. The Hospitals Cup remained in the hands of the recently created Imperial Medicals team, albeit through a narrow 19-17 victory over the Guy's, King's and St Thomas's combination. The Army were the Services champions again after a narrow win over the Royal Air Force and a splendid performance against the Royal Navy at Twickenham for a 32-14 win in a match which attracted an estimated crowd of 30,000. The airmen had started off their campaign against the Navy, losing comfortably in poor conditions at Portsmouth.

Those who predict the demise of the Barbarians were again confounded, as the club won five fixtures out of six, losing only at Coventry. These results included narrow end-of-season victories over enthusiastic but understrength Ireland and Scotland teams and a scintillating display at Twickenham in which the Barbarians demolished champions Leicester 85-10. The last-mentioned match deserves a place on the fixture list, but would it not be better to present it as an early season hors d'oeuvre rather than as a postscript against a club side probably playing one game too many? However, the fact that the Barbarians continue to thrive is a tribute to the superb way Geoff Windsor-Lewis manages to organise matters on the club's behalf and shows that plenty of fans still exist who respect the finer traditions of the game.

The two finals for minor junior clubs were played at Twickenham on a damp afternoon. In the Vase there was success for Sheffield Tigers against the Bank of England. The latter failed to turn early superiority into a winning advantage and subsequently made too many handling errors against a doughty Yorkshire outfit. The NPI Cup final, meanwhile, resulted in another triumph for unbeaten Dunstablians during an *annus mirabilis* which has seen them rewarded with promotion to senior status, where their future fortunes will arouse great interest. In a rain-affected final and by a narrow margin (14-10), their victims were Hull Ionians, another ambitious club.

The Middlesex Sevens were postponed to the new season, which is probably a good move, since, as we hinted earlier, the battery of end-of-season activities has become too much of a good thing. In my own case, I declared at the end of May. In future would it not be a good idea to make that a final cut-off point? Otherwise players will become really stale, and touring personnel may also be badly affected. Some people also like to have summer holidays, and the fact that many are professionals does not mean that they should be driven into the ground.

Another hobby horse of mine is the gradual erosion of traditional values. Couldn't we go back to having the previous season's Oxbridge captains as touch judges at the Varsity Match? And what was wrong with Inter-Services matches being controlled by officials from the union which was not involved in a particular contest? These were decent traditions which have been forsaken for no good reason. Their abandonment is a symptom of a desire for change where none is necessary. By all means be ambitious, but please respect the game's traditions. Because we have a professional – it should really be called 'open' – game, it does not mean that cynicism should take over from decent standards. But if the asinine 'entertainment' at the Tetley's Bitter final, which must also be endured at some club matches, is any guide, it looks as if such undesirable nonsense is already with us.

Trevor Walsh of Premiership newcomers Henley shrugs off Worcester's Andrew Higgins during their September clash at Dry Leas. Henley finished the season just below halfway, while Worcester, in their second Premiership season, finished third for the second year in succession, and along with Leeds Tykes made Rotherham fight for their title.

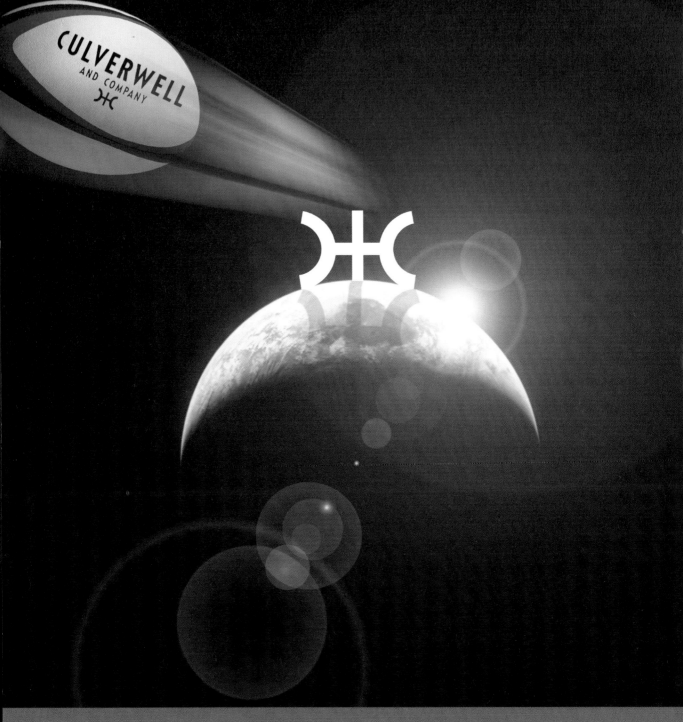

SCOTLAND – Striking a balance

BY ALAN LORIMER

Walk into any clubhouse in Scotland just prior to a league match these days and the chances are you'll see a large group of folk crowding round the TV set. Their focus of attention is usually a televised match from the Allied Dunbar Premiership, a chance to see professional club rugby in a country where that sector remains predominantly amateur. Of course not all rugby in Scotland is about shunning money. The professional side of Scottish rugby resides in the two so-called Superdistricts, Edinburgh Reivers and Glasgow Caledonians, both financed and controlled by the Scottish Rugby Union and both major suppliers of players to the Scotland and Scotland A sides.

Not everyone sees this as the best route for professionalism in Scotland. There remain a number of vocal critics, the rump of the last rebellion, who claim that the Superdistricts have destroyed club rugby while at the same time have shown few tangible returns from the sizeable investment made in them by the Scottish Rugby Union. These detractors suggest that instead of pouring money into 'artificial' teams that have little or no natural fan base, the funds would be better used in creating a professional club-based system. It is an argument that will continue, but for the moment, and with the endorsement of the Lord Mackay review panel, Superdistricts are the preferred option for delivering a professional layer to Scotland. So much so that the talk is now of creating a third professional district based in the Scottish Borders.

For the Scottish Rugby Union the task of simultaneously managing the professional and amateur games will always be a delicate balancing act. The interface of these two seemingly disparate codes is the first division of the Premiership, and it is here that the bridge between professionalism and amateurism can be created. Jim Telfer, the SRU director of rugby, believes that the standard in the first division of the Premiership must be raised so that the gulf between the amateur and professional players can be narrowed. To achieve this end, the SRU may have to apply financial means by injecting enough cash to make the top end of the Premiership semi-professional.

Meanwhile, for the full-time pros, the 1999-2000 season was never going to be easy. This was the first season that Scotland's professional players were exposed to the real world of professional rugby, which in the northern hemisphere means a large diet of games. Last season the Scottish and Welsh Unions agreed the setting-up of a league in which the two Superdistricts would join 12 clubs from Wales in a home-and-away competition that would generate 22 games for each side. In the event it was a learning process for the Scottish sides, who, perhaps handicapped by the excessive amount of travelling entailed by a logistically difficult competition, finished in the bottom half of the league. But amid the gloomy statistics (which provided further ammunition for the critics of the Superdistricts) there were enough in the way of good results to suggest that a further season of bedding in can only mean better results in the future.

Among these good results were the home wins over Swansea and Llanelli by Edinburgh Reivers, whose strong run at the end of the league, under coach Bob Easson, can only give hope for the future. Reivers, however, are not relying on hope but rather on the efforts they have made to strengthen their squad. To this end, Reivers have signed up a number of Scotland and Scotland A players hitherto based south of the border.

WOODEN SPOON SOCIETY RUGBY WORLD '01

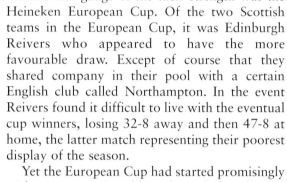

Among the high-profile players to sign up are the Northampton pair Richard Metcalfe and Don Mackinnon, the Scotland and Leicester outside back Craig Joiner and the Harlequins centre David Officer.

Reivers, like their Glasgow counterparts, have also sought to increase the size of their playing squad, the lesson learned from last season being that survival in a tough league depends on quantity just as much as quality. The hidden agenda in the recruitment of players like Metcalfe would seem to be that of fulfilling the desire of Telfer and Scotland coach Ian McGeechan to have as many as possible of the national players based north of the border. The signing by Glasgow Caledonians of James McLaren from the French club Bourgoin-Jallieu served only to confirm this theory.

If the Welsh Scottish League gave an indication of how the Reivers and the Reds could survive in a season-long competition, then the real gauge of the their strength was the

Edinburgh and Scotland back Chris Paterson is tackled by Swansea's Mark Taylor during the Scottish Superdistrict's home win over the Welsh club in the Welsh Scottish League.

Heineken European Cup. Of the two Scottish teams in the European Cup, it was Edinburgh Reivers who appeared to have the more favourable draw. Except of course that they shared company in their pool with a certain English club called Northampton. In the event Reivers found it difficult to live with the eventual cup winners, losing 32-8 away and then 47-8 at home, the latter match representing their poorest display of the season.

Yet the European Cup had started promisingly with wins over Grenoble and Neath, but the two defeats by Northampton in successive games were the killer blows. Reivers still had a chance of making it to the quarter-finals after defeating Neath 23-20 at the Gnoll, but against Grenoble they were well short of achieving the necessary points total for a place in the last eight.

Glasgow Caledonians can reflect on two Euro successes, achieving victories over Leinster and Leicester, which showed that they can live with the best. But away from home the Reds disappointed. They, too, will be hoping that a stronger and enlarged squad can bring better results at both league and cup levels.

In the amateur game it was Heriot's FP who set the early pace and who had the stamina to finish as winners of the BT Scotland Premiership with a dynamic brand of rugby that was as effective as it was entertaining. Key to Heriot's successful defence of their title was the form of stand-off Gordon Ross, whose astute tactical judgment, accurate goal-kicking and overall generalship brought out the best from a talented back division that had pace in the back three of Gregor Lawson, Stewart Walker and Charlie

Keenan and strength at centre in Hugh Gilmour. Heriot's other major success was No. 8 Simon Taylor, who, like Ross, was rewarded with an Edinburgh Reivers contract for this season.

On paper, Glasgow Hawks should have challenged Heriot's much more closely, but in the event the Anniesland side never maintained the consistency necessary for league success. Both players and coaches at Hawks pointed out the difficulties they had training at Anniesland during the worst of the winter months, when the mud became so deep that scrum halves were in danger of permanently disappearing. Hawks, needless to say, are advocates of summer rugby.

Once again it was Melrose who carried Border hopes of a title win, but in the crunch matches the Greenyards men were unable to meet the challenge, their third-place finish representing unfulfilled potential. Coach Gary Parker rightly suggested that last year was

More Welsh Scottish League action, this time from the clash between Glasgow Caledonians and Newport. Here the Glasgow full back, Rowen Shepherd, is tackled by Jason Foster.

'a season too early' for his young side. The talent is there. It simply needs another season to mature. Melrose, however, discovered a talented stand-off in Callum Macrae, a Scotland U21 cap this season, and with former Hawick scrum half Rob Chrystie hitting fine form the Greenyards team have a useful half-back partnership.

Youth was the theme at Hawick, where under coach Ian Barnes the Greens if not reviving the glory days of the 1970s certainly showed that rugby is still a major part of the Border culture. Their best win was against Hawks, a victory that effectively ended the Glasgow side's title challenge.

It was never going to be easy for Gala, who having won the Division Two title and the cup in the 1998-99 season promptly paid for their success by losing all their top players to professional rugby. Gala, however, seemed to overcome these difficulties and after a good start led the Premiership at one stage, only to slip rapidly down the table before a late recovery lodged them in fifth position.

At Riverside Park, Jed-Forest have become a synonym for home-grown product. The Royal Blues have worked incredibly hard to nurture local talent and last season, despite finishing in the lower half of the league, Jed's policy proved its worth with a number of memorable wins over the likes of Heriot's and Melrose.

For the Borders to sustain five clubs in the first division was never viable. In the event the rise and fall of Kelso proved the point, the Poynder Park side struggling throughout the league campaign before being relegated to Division Two along with West of Scotland.

Elsewhere, Currie, who finished in fourth spot, retained their place among the top Scottish clubs, but there was a disappointing season for Watsonians, who at one stage were dangerously close to the relegation zone.

Boroughmuir, winners of the BT Cellnet Cup and champions of the second division of the BT Scotland Premiership.

In Division Two Boroughmuir dominated from start to finish to prove that their one and only season in the second tier was little more than a blip in their distinguished history. As with Gala a year before, Boroughmuir completed the double by adding the BT Cellnet Cup title to their second division success with an unexpectedly large victory by 35-10 over Glasgow Hawks in the final at Murrayfield.

The challenge for the amateur game is to improve on the standard of rugby it achieved last season. Club rugby must also be backed by the powers that be, not least because in an era when schools rugby is disappearing at an alarming rate it is the clubs who must take over the teaching role and with it the role of securing the future of the game.

WALES – The Llanelli revival

BY **DAVID STEWART**

'Yield not to temptation, for yielding is sin... ' goes the refrain sung in the gospel halls of Wales. One must assume Llanelli's Ian Boobyer is not a regular attendee at his local Pentecostal. On a sunny Sunday in May at the Madejski Stadium, with extra time beckoning, he lay at the base of a ruck as the ball emerged on the Northampton side. Dom Malone was on the field as replacement for England captain Matt Dawson. He prepared to pass, and the temptation for the wing forward was too much to resist. Penalty, Paul Grayson, three points, game over, the termination of Llanelli's European adventure, and Northampton on the way to Twickenham and victory in the Heineken Cup final.

Acrobatics from Llanelli's Simon Easterby (wtih ball) and Northampton's Federico Mendez at the Madejski Stadium, Reading. Llanelli ran the Saints close in this European Cup semi-final but could not quite prevail.

As one rugby century rolled into another it was a sign of the changing times and the prominence of the five-year-old competition that this represented the biggest game for any Welsh club during the season – if that term is still appropriate for something that now lasts for a ten-month period from August to May. This epic period was dominated by Wales hosting Rugby World Cup 1999, centred upon the fabulous and (just about) completed Millennium Stadium. Other lasting memories are likely to be the 'Grannygate' eligibility affair, the ending of Graham Henry's extended honeymoon period and the revival of Llanelli, who won the Welsh Rugby Union Challenge Cup for the eleventh time as some compensation for their brave and thrilling but ultimately doomed bid for success in European competition. Their status as the leading club of the moment is a measure of the improvement Gareth Jenkins has wrought in a continuing period of service as player and coach stretching back some 30 years. That he has achieved this with a commitment and enthusiasm that belies any element of staleness and with only modest financial resources at his disposal was recognised by his inclusion in the shortlist of those under consideration to take the Lions to Australia in 2001.

Llanelli struggled to come to terms with the professional era, and at one stage the WRU had to bail them out by purchasing Stradey Park. As the financing of leading Welsh clubs has settled down, linked to a formula based on qualification for the European Cup, Llanelli, in common with others, have been able to engage in the relative luxury of planning for at least the medium term. Jenkins and his talent spotters had chosen well when utilising the playing budget in the previous close season. Richmond's demise brought prop John Davies and local boy Scott Quinnell back to West Wales, and less noticeably second row Craig Gillies. His dominant line-out performances and scoring of crucial tries in the European quarter-final against Cardiff and the domestic cup final against Swansea made him the find of the season. Not far behind was back-row forward Simon Easterby, whose progress was recognised by the Irish selectors.

Other useful acquisitions were prop Phil Booth from Cardiff and centre/wing Salesi Finau, who is one of those Tongan gentlemen with an instinct for what certain commentators refer to as 'over-robust play'. Indeed he was lucky to be on duty in the Northampton match, having been sent off for 'head-hunting' the previous week. In the semi-final, Booth shared the dunce's hat with Boobyer when he earned ten minutes in the sin-bin following his barnhouse attack on Tim Rodber, albeit in response to provocation. However, his progress from Arms Park reserve to Wales Development Squad member for their tour to Canada mirrored that of Easterby, being an illustration of the club's ability to develop players. This included turning Matt Cardey into a full international full back. The ex-Newport player, whose running and hairstyle both attract the adjective 'flamboyant', was capped against Scotland and, unlike some when the brouhaha started, was able to prove a grandparentage within the Principality. That international also saw a debut by home-bred out-half Stephen Jones, who was partnered on the day by Rupert Moon, making an unexpected return to Welsh colours. With his inspiration, commitment to the club and its supporters and a mutual admiration society with his coach, Moon will continue at the Llanelli helm for at least one more year. He claims to relish the competition from Guy Easterby, Simon's brother, who signed from Ebbw Vale and was capped during Ireland's summer tour. Another exciting newcomer from the mid-Wales nursery of Builth Wells is wing Mark Jones, who was invited by Graham Henry to show his paces in the end-of-season fixture against the French Barbarians.

The new millennium saw the first cup final held in the Millennium Stadium (as it is currently named) and it brought sweet revenge for Llanelli. A year earlier Swansea had beaten them at Ninian Park, and after a season of playing friendly matches against English clubs Scott Gibbs rubbed Scarlet noses in the dirt when saying that he had found the opposition 'softer' that day than he had been used to. The 2000 final was a less than enchanting game but saw Swansea beaten 22-12. The losers also had a frustrating time upon their return to league rugby in the new Welsh-Scottish competition, when their fancied squad could finish no better than third. This was sufficient to qualify them for another season in the financially rewarding European Cup, but the failure to win a trophy will have frustrated the St Helens faithful. Centre Mark Taylor was their leading performer and his progress at international level was recognised with the captaincy of Wales against the French BaaBaas. Gibbs will stand down from that role at Swansea, but after the usual speculation about whether he would return to Rugby League or play elsewhere, he will be sticking around for the new term. With Darren Morris, Garin Jenkins, Ben Evans and Colin Charvis forming the core of a pack seeking to feed runners of the calibre of Arwel Thomas and Kevin Morgan, the absence of silverware need not continue.

Cardiff won the new league competition. It had a somewhat unsatisfactory air and a feeling of transience. The observation is intended to apply to the competition but is equally relevant to its winners. Their chairman, Peter Thomas, and his Swansea counterpart fought a doughty battle to join the Allied Dunbar clubs before the English RFU closed off that option. The political shenanigans between the latter body and its clubs represented by English First Division Rugby are documented elsewhere. A British League may seem the natural progression for most supporters in Wales, and in the race to maintain top-level playing standards they have the support of the union based in Cardiff but not the one in southwest London, at least not yet.

Liam Botham, a tourist to South Africa with England, in action for Cardiff against Harlequins in the European Cup. Botham has now returned to England to play his club rugby.

Being the big city club and the richest one to boot, Cardiff are frequently the subject of envy and criticism from their rivals. Accordingly, some consider their league victory is tarnished by the differential points system used in World Cup year. With their own ground closed before the tournament while the builders were finishing next door, all their early games were played away when a win was worth two points only, leaving an excess of home games at a value of four points. Success in an unsponsored and thus not terribly lucrative competition brings its own disappointments in the professional era. If indeed the litmus test is European, a quarter-final defeat at Stradey Park by 22-3 in a particularly insipid display registers as unsatisfactory. A few players, including Liam Botham, have left to play in England, but a strong squad remains, spearheaded by Rob Howley and Neil Jenkins and supported by the fast-improving Williams boys – Martyn at wing forward and Rhys at full back.

The most significant newcomer to the club scene was former Springbok captain Gary Teichmann. He was appointed captain of Newport shortly after his arrival and galvanised them to second place. This represented the best return on the part of this famous old club for some two decades. The funds injected by businessman Tony Brown, who runs the show as chief executive, enabled the recruitment of internationals Peter Rogers, David Llewellyn and the unfortunate Shane Howarth, whose contributions towards the season's end, often from out-half, were in the midst of his well-publicised family tree difficulties. Allen Lewis will continue to coach the club as well as assisting Graham Henry. He will have additional power in the front five following the recruitment of Adrian Garvey from Natal and Ian Gough returning from Pontypridd. The latter have also lost fellow Welsh international forward Geraint Lewis to Swansea. The loss of such quality players on the heels of Neil Jenkins and others a year earlier bodes ill for Pontypridd's chances of staying in the top five as they did this time, confirming another European Cup qualification. If nothing else, they will hope for a trouble-free encounter with their next French opponents. Following on from Ponty's infamous battles with Brive, in last year's home fixture against Colomiers, the French club's prop Richard Nones was dismissed for eye-gouging.

The hard luck story of the year was undoubtedly Ebbw Vale. Their leading light off the field is locally born Marcus Russell, who is better known as manager of the notorious Oasis band. Few would quibble that his commitment deserved better than the frustrations of the club's losing to London Irish with the last kick of their European Shield quarter-final contest. After this came defeat by Llanelli in the Challenge Cup semi-finals, and the ultimate disappointment was losing 13-12 to Bridgend in the last league game, which meant they slipped to sixth place and another year in the Shield rather than the more lucrative Cup. That picture is brightened considerably by the acquisition of one of the best Welsh coaches available in Mike Ruddock. His return to the Gwent Valley from Leinster has been supported by the WRU, who have confirmed him in a three-year term as coach of the Welsh A side. Conventional wisdom suggests this marks his grooming as Henry's successor, given a solid performance in both jobs. The smart money suggests that might just be after the Lions tour rather than the 2003 World Cup. Neutrals would not fault the New Zealander for his evident disillusionment midway through the Six Nations when the professional critics got rather carried away and induced the resignation of his close confidant Steve Black.

It is happening slowly, but the organisation of the game in Wales is definitely moving in favour of the national team, something Henry called for shortly after his arrival. Only Allan Bateman of the best players still plays in England. The better players are concentrating, with WRU blessing, around the strongest five or six clubs. The gap between those and the minnows is massive, witnessed by Cardiff's destruction of relegated Dunvant by 106-0. That result led Peter Thomas to raise the alarm for the safety of part-time players competing regularly against bigger, stronger, fitter and more experienced men. It is quite understandable that the likes of promoted Cross Keys want to play against the strongest clubs. Before departing, Ebbw Vale's Richard Hill expressed the view that the Glasgow and Edinburgh teams had not been fully interested in the competition. Whatever the destiny of the proposed British Cup, surely a British League is an inevitable development. For the game to continue developing, it needs investment. That the two main existing domestic competitions cannot attract sponsors speaks for itself. In a slightly different way, so does the union's desire to sell the name of the new stadium to the highest corporate bidder. The great irony in an age of devolved government is that Welsh club rugby needs its English neighbours, who in turn are being slow to see the mutual attraction.

IRELAND – St Mary's year

BY SEAN DIFFLEY

St Mary's College captain Trevor Brennan hoists the All Ireland League trophy. The Dublin side finished top of the table, then beat Ballymena in the semifinals before defeating Lansdowne in the final.

It had to end sometime, the monopoly of the All Ireland League by Munster clubs, but in the final stages of the competition in May 2000, nary a Munster side was to be seen. Instead the competition was fought out by three clubs from Leinster and one from Ulster, with the Dublin side, St Mary's College, emerging victorious. So no sign of Shannon, no sign of Young Munster or Garryowen or the holders, Cork Constitution. The Munster sides, you see, had other thoughts in mind.

There is no doubt that the calls of the Munster provincial side and their glorious path in the Heineken European Cup tended to impinge on the concentration of the clubs in the south. For instance, scrum half Peter Stringer of Shannon and fly half Ronan O'Gara of Cork Constitution were the new half-back pairing and the linchpin of the Munster team and its progress in Europe; they were also part of Ireland's renaissance in the latter part of the Six Nations, which saw the first Ireland win in Paris for 28 years and the revival of hope for the future. And with such as Mick Galwey of Shannon, Keith Wood (on his year's 'leave' from Harlequins) of Garryowen and Peter Clohessy of Young Munster so often otherwise engaged, the emphasis was not as firmly set on the AIL as in all previous years.

Yet there is a fair volume of opinion that a change from the dominance of Munster clubs would have come about anyway. Even before Munster had begun to reach the giddier heights in Europe there were indications that the old order could be about to change. In the end St Mary's on the season's evidence were worthy of the distinction of champion club. And – as they would be the first to say – about time, too! Too often in recent times they had flattered to deceive. Trips to Munster too often resulted in quite humiliating reverses. The previous season, for instance, they were into the semi-finals and led Garryowen by 17 points in the first half, only to collapse embarrassingly and go out. Was some malignant spirit up there ensuring that St Mary's would never beat a Munster team in Munster? As it happened, this past season saw the exorcism of the bad spirit, and St Mary's won with some fine displays and with renewed exhibitions of character.

The format of the competition is that it is played on a league basis, with the top four teams of the twelve then taking part in knock-out play-offs, or semi-finals. St Mary's topped the league and played their semi-final against the fourth-placed side, which was Ballymena. Second-placed Lansdowne had their semi-final engagement with the third-placed club, which was Terenure College.

Mary's, led by that craggy Ireland flanker Trevor Brennan and with such as wing Denis Hickie and No. 8 Victor Costello in the side, faced a Ballymena team that had made a late run. Ballymena had David Humphreys and Dion O'Cuinneagain in a team that was locked in close combat on the St Mary's ground until the second half, when a classy St Mary's emerged convincing winners. In the other match, Lansdowne were clear winners over Terenure, but the final, unfortunately, was a rather dull affair. Mary's never really revealed their real form, but what they showed was good enough to win.

And it was a popular win, since St Mary's are noted down the years for playing the open, entertaining brand of football. Among the Lions to wear the all-blue jersey are Ciaran Fitzgerald the 1983 captain in New Zealand, Tony Ward, Paul Dean, Sean Lynch,

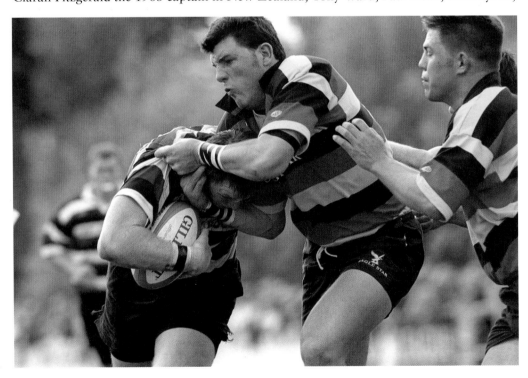

All Ireland League semi-final action. Lansdowne's Shane Horgan tackles Eric Miller of Terenure College.

Munster fly half Ronan O'Gara, of the Cork Constitution club and Ireland, takes on Toulouse scrum half Jérome Cazalbou. The Irish province triumphed 31-25 over the French club to qualify for the European Cup final, where they were narrowly defeated by Northampton.

Tom Grace, John Moloney, and Vincent Cunningham. Four of these players also captained Ireland.

But of course the passage of Munster in the European Cup tended to relegate most other things to the background. It was an extraordinary episode and the irony of it was that Munster, so often in the past the epitome of the dogged game of attrition, the inventors of the 'garryowen', played some of the most creative rugby of the competition. Munster may have been beaten by a single point by Northampton, but they lost no caste at all. That they contributed so much to that huge crowd of 66,441 at Twickenham for the final is to their eternal credit. And the atmosphere at Twickenham that day was one of the greatest shots in the arm that the game has had since the introduction of the code of professionalism. Paid football it may be, but the old spirit still survives.

As Robert Kitson wrote in the *Guardian*, '... far more relevant, if rugby knows what is good for it, were the overlapping strands of grace, dignity, humility and honesty that were interwoven into the tapestry', or as David Hands wrote in *The Times*, 'If the administrators want to package an image of the sport in the new millennium, let them do so around the players and spectators at Twickenham on Saturday,' as, at the final whistle, as Mick Cleary pointed out in the *Daily Telegraph*, 'the teams and supporters alike mingled and shared their respective joy and sorrow'.

All that – plus Ulster's win the previous year when English clubs did not participate and the competition's future looked doubtful – highlights the philosophy of Declan Kidney, the quiet but so effective Munster coach. 'The trouble with a lot of Irish sport is a national feeling of inadequacy, of lack of confidence. I believe that there is more talent and ability than we realise. When you are self-confident, the result is success. Doubt is the forerunner of defeat,' says Kidney.

FRANCE – Player power wins

BY **CHRIS THAU**

Stade Français captain Christophe Juillet in action during his side's 1999-2000 Heineken Cup clash with Leicester at Welford Road. Said Juillet of the coach situation that preceded the French Championship final, 'In the end we did not know who coached whom, but it was an extraordinary experience.'

It is always a matter of opinion with the French. If you read the papers, the French Championship final between Stade Français and Colomiers was a disaster, with half of the 80,000-seat Stade de France empty. While acknowledging that the capacity crowd at the previous ground, Parc des Princes, was under 50,000, leading French rugby weekly *Midi Olympique* described the game as 'the final of indifference', arguing that a combination of post-World Cup fatigue, the timing of the match (it was the latest final ever held, virtually in the middle of the French holiday season), over-saturation on TV (the match was broadcast by two stations), and FFR–Stade de France differences led to the poor attendance figures.

While all this is, of course, a matter of opinion, many of the arguments could well be true, and the post-mortem will undoubtedly reveal the cause of the alleged 'indifference'. On the other hand, if you were one of the lucky 45,000 who did attend, you may have left with a different opinion at the end of an electrifying match of high drama and emotion. The fashionable Stade Français, one of the oldest French clubs (they were the losing finalists in the first French Championship in 1892) beat newcomers Colomiers (formed in 1963 in one of the Toulouse working-class satellite neighbourhoods) 28-23 in the final match of the longest season in French rugby history.

After convincingly despatching Stade Toulousain, the Rolls-Royce of French clubs, 30-13 in the semi-finals, the cosmopolitan Parisians went on to both confound and delight the pundits further by winning the coveted Bouclier de Brennus, the championship trophy, on 15 July in Paris. The win surprised the media because Stade Français had been without a coach since a players 'revolt' led to the early departure of coach Georges Coste in May.

Coste, who managed to take Italy from the ranks of Europe's also-rans to a place in the Six Nations, was hastily brought in by club owner Max Guazzini following the appointment of former club coach Bernard Laporte as national coach after the World Cup. It is believed that Coste's no-nonsense, disciplinarian approach when faced with a group of mature, well-versed players led to the uprising, which ended with his abrupt departure. Coste, one of the world's most accomplished and innovative coaches, stepped aside with dignity, refusing to blame anybody for the debacle, while, significantly, the players have restated their respect for Coste both in public and private.

The fact is that the team entered the knock-out stages without a coach, the technical and administrative interim being secured by two young assistants, Eric Bachoffer and Alain Elias, and with two senior players, Diego Dominguez and Fabrice Landreau, taking over the coaching duties. As a result, as often happens in these circumstances, the events helped concentrate the minds of the players, who may have been concerned that the whole episode might backfire.

The promotion of Bernard Laporte (above) to the post of national coach after the World Cup brought Georges Coste to Stade Français. The former Italy coach stayed only until May, however, and Stade were coachless by the time of the championship final in July.

'In the end we did not know who coached whom, but it was an extraordinary experience,' Stade Français captain Christophe Julliet said. The players trained for hours, and Landreau's insistence on scrummaging practice paid off in the final, when the difference between the virile challenge of the Parisians in the scrum and the indifferent performance of the Colomiers pack made the difference between tears of joy and despair.

Meanwhile, at the other end of the scale the streamlining exercise in the 22-strong French premier division is on course, with the 2000-01 season as the final test for those 16 clubs keen to remain among the elite. At the time of writing, Toulon RFC, one of the leading lights of French rugby in the 1980s, have been declared relegated to the second division – which is also professional – but the charismatic club president, former international scrum half Jerome Gallion, hopes to be able to successfully appeal against the FFR decision.

The management of the league decided not to replace Toulon, leaving only 21 clubs, divided into two pools of 10 and 11 respectively, in the premier division for the next season, with a 12-strong second division. One of the big names of French rugby, Graulhet, have dropped out of sight and are now playing in one of the feeder pools of the lower, amateur structure.

ITALY – Revenge of the Romans

BY **CHRIS THAU**

The unexpected outcome of the Italian league has somewhat baffled the Italian public, but for the experienced observer the success of eventual winners Rugby Roma, as well as the presence of their neighbours from L'Aquila in the final, has not come as a surprise. Roma, under French coach Gilbert Doucet, have been quietly building up since last season, following a period of mixed fortunes in the recent history of the club.

However, the arrival from Cordoba in Argentina of the youthful Ramiro Pez changed the fortunes of Roma. Pez, who played for Diego Dominguez's former club La Tablada, was the catalyst that led to the eventual Roman 'revolution'. The fly half joined Roma just before the final round of play-offs, and his impact was instantaneous. Roma suddenly graduated from being one of the challengers to a leading role, which culminated in the demolition of aspiring champions Viadana 42-19 in the semi-finals. In the final, the Rome club rampaged to a 30-0 lead at half-time, then slowed down to win 35-17 and claim their first title in more than 50 years.

BenettonTreviso, arguably the best known Italian club, believed too much in their own press, which argued that a win by anything less than 20 points against L'Aquila in the semi-finals (Treviso having beaten them by 50 points in the play-offs) would be regarded as a poor showing. It is difficult to say whether Treviso's premature dreams of glory were the main factor in the narrow 19-17 defeat, or whether it was the hard-nosed expertise of L'Aquila's new player-coach Mike Brewer, who was able to turn a moderate squad into

The influence of their new player-coach, former All Black back-row forward Mike Brewer, seen here with West Hartlepool, may have contributed to L'Aquila's victory over Benetton Treviso in the semi-finals.

Padova, along with Benetton Treviso, participated in the 1999-2000 Heineken European Cup, finding themselves in the same group as Bath. Here Padova's Corrado Covi tackles Matt Perry during the encounter at the Rec.

a winning outfit for what was arguably L'Aquila's most important match in decades. The victory secured the former champions a lucrative berth in Europe, in Pool 2 of the Heineken Cup alongside Swansea and Wasps and French champions Stade Français. Roma, meanwhile, are in Pool 5 and will take on the likes of Llanelli, Colomiers and Gloucester.

In fairness to Treviso, who will have to taste life in the European Shield for the first time, one could argue that the structure of the Italian league is conducive to the hit-and-run tactics employed by the L'Aquila club. After the early home-and-away rounds, the 12-team premier division is divided into two pools of six – the top six clubs play among themselves home and away to determine the four semi-finalists, while the bottom six follow a similar pattern to decide the two clubs to be relegated; this year it was Calvisano and Bologna. Once the top four clubs are determined, and this season they were, in descending order, Treviso, Viadana, Roma and L'Aquila, it all becomes a matter of taking one match at a time.

The winners of the second division, Gran Parma, the second club in the city after Parma RFC, plus Silea won the right to play in the first division next season. Meanwhile, most clubs are making stringent financial cuts, trying to tailor their ambitions to their means. The exercise will be very difficult, in some cases quite painful, and will involve some of the better-known names in Italian rugby. Two of the clubs said to be experiencing financial difficulties are former champions Rovigo and Petrarca Padua.

A SUMMARY OF THE SEASON 1999-2000

BY BILL MITCHELL

RUGBY WORLD CUP 1999

GROUP A

Spain	15	Uruguay			27
Scotland	29	South Africa			46
Scotland	43	Uruguay			12
South Africa	47	Spain			3
South Africa	39	Uruguay			3
Scotland	48	Spain			0

	P	W	L	F	A	Pts
South Africa	3	3	0	132	35	9
Scotland	3	2	1	120	58	7
Uruguay	3	1	2	42	97	5
Spain	3	0	3	18	122	3

GROUP B

England	67	Italy			7
New Zealand	45	Tonga			9
England	14	New Zealand			30
Italy	25	Tonga			28
New Zealand	101	Italy			0
England	101	Tonga			10

	P	W	L	F	A	Pts
New Zealand	3	3	0	176	28	9
England	3	2	1	184	47	7
Tonga	3	1	2	47	171	5
Italy	3	0	3	35	196	3

GROUP C

Fiji	67	Namibia			18
France	33	Canada			20
France	47	Namibia			13
Fiji	38	Canada			22
Canada	72	Namibia			11
France	28	Fiji			19

	P	W	L	F	A	Pts
France	3	3	0	108	52	9
Fiji	3	2	1	122	68	7
Canada	3	1	2	114	82	5
Namibia	3	0	3	42	186	3

GROUP D

Wales	23	Argentina			18
Japan	9	Samoa			43
Wales	64	Japan			15
Argentina	32	Samoa			16
Wales	31	Samoa			38
Argentina	33	Japan			12

	P	W	L	F	A	Pts
Wales	3	2	1	118	71	7
Samoa	3	2	1	97	72	7
Argentina	3	2	1	83	51	7
Japan	3	0	3	36	140	3

GROUP E

Ireland	53	United States			8
Australia	57	Romania			9
United States	25	Romania			27
Ireland	3	Australia			23
Australia	55	United States			19
Ireland	44	Romania			14

	P	W	L	F	A	Pts
Australia	3	3	0	135	31	9
Ireland	3	2	1	100	45	7
Romania	3	1	2	50	126	5
United States	3	0	3	52	135	3

KNOCK-OUT STAGES

Quarter-final Play-offs

England	45	Fiji	24
Scotland	35	Samoa	20
Ireland	24	Argentina	28

Quarter-finals

Wales	9	Australia	24
South Africa	44	England	21
France	47	Argentina	26
Scotland	18	New Zealand	30

Semi-finals

Australia	27	South Africa	21
France	43	New Zealand	31

Third-place Play-off

New Zealand	18	South Africa	22

Final

Australia	35	France	12

INTERNATIONAL RUGBY

ENGLAND IN SOUTH AFRICA
JUNE 2000

Opponents	Results
North West Leopards	W 52-22
SOUTH AFRICA	L 13-18
Griqualand West	W 55-16
SOUTH AFRICA	W 27-22
Gauteng Falcons	W 36-27

Played 5 Won 4 Lost 1

SCOTLAND IN NEW ZEALAND
JUNE & JULY 2000

Opponents	Results
Northland	L 16-42
East Coast/Poverty Bay	W 51-10
New Zealand Maori	L 15-18
Nelson-Bays	D 25-25
NEW ZEALAND	L 20-69
Hawke's Bay	W 24-7
NEW ZEALAND	L 14-48

Played 7 Won 2 Drawn 1 Lost 4

WALES DEVELOPMENT SQUAD
IN CANADA
JUNE & JULY 2000

Opponents	Results
Eastern Canada	W 19-0
Ontario	W 19-13
Canada 'A'	W 67-10
Young Canada	W 32-17
British Columbia XV	W 72-22

Played 5 Won 5

IRELAND IN THE AMERICAS
JUNE 2000

Opponents	Results
ARGENTINA	L 23-34
UNITED STATES	W 83-3
CANADA	D 27-27

Played 3 Won 1 Drawn 1 Lost 1

ARGENTINA IN AUSTRALIA
JUNE 2000

Opponents	Results
Queensland	W 35-29
AUSTRALIA	L 6-53

Played 2 Won 1 Lost 1

ITALY IN SAMOA AND FIJI
JUNE 2000

Opponents	Results
Samoa 'A'	L 26-29
Samoa	L 24-43
Fiji	L 9-13

Played 3 Lost 3

LLOYDS TSB SIX NATIONS
CHAMPIONSHIP 2000

Results

England	50	Ireland	18
Italy	34	Scotland	20
Wales	3	France	31
France	9	England	15
Ireland	44	Scotland	22
Wales	47	Italy	16
England	46	Wales	12
Ireland	60	Italy	13
Scotland	16	France	28
Italy	12	England	59
Wales	26	Scotland	18
France	25	Ireland	27
France	42	Italy	31
Ireland	19	Wales	23
Scotland	19	England	13

	P	W	L	F	A	Pts
England	5	4	1	183	70	8
France	5	3	2	142	94	6
Ireland	5	3	2	168	133	6
Wales	5	3	2	111	135	6
Scotland	5	1	4	95	145	2
Italy	5	1	4	106	228	2

OTHER INTERNATIONALS &
REPRESENTATIVE MATCHES

RUGBY WORLD CUP WARM-UP MATCHES

England 'A'	54	United States	6
Scotland 'A'	25	Argentina 'A'	25
Scotland	22	Argentina	31
Wales	33	Canada	19
England	106	United States	8
Leinster	22	Argentina	51
Scotland	60	Romania	19
Wales	34	France	23
Ireland	32	Argentina	24
England	36	Canada	11
Wales XV	53	United States	24
England XV	67	Premiership XV	14
Munster	26	Ireland XV	15
England XV	92	P'ship All Stars	17
Ulster	16	Ireland XV	25
Glasgow C'donians	3	Scotland XV	53

TOGETHER WE CAN BUILD A BETTER FUTURE

We are proud to support the Wooden Spoon Society

PRICEWATERHOUSE COPERS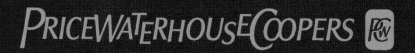

www.pwcglobal.com

ASIAN CHAMPIONSHIPS (HELD IN JAPAN)

Final Placements
1. Japan
2. Korea
3. Taiwan
4. Hong Kong
5. Singapore
6. China
7. Sri Lanka
8. Thailand

OTHER

Scotland 'A'	99	Holland	0
South Africa	51	Canada	18
New Zealand	102	Tonga	0
South Africa	51	Canada	18
Wales	40	French B'barians	33
Australia	44	South Africa	23

(Nelson Mandela Trophy)

SIX NATIONS 'A' CHAMPIONSHIP

Results

England	30	Ireland	31
Italy	16	Scotland	23
Wales	30	France	24
France	26	England	20
Ireland	23	Scotland	21
Wales	43	Italy	16
England	19	Wales	14
Ireland	31	Italy	3
Scotland	38	France	34
Italy	27	England	33
Wales	30	Scotland	23
France	31	Ireland	25
France	29	Italy	18
Ireland	28	Wales	26
Scotland	31	England	34

	P	W	L	F	A	Pts
Ireland	5	4	1	138	111	8
Wales	5	3	2	143	113	6
France	5	3	2	147	131	6
England	5	3	2	136	129	6
Scotland	5	2	3	136	137	4
Italy	5	0	5	80	159	0

UNDER 21 INTERNATIONAL RESULTS

SIX NATIONS

England	20	Ireland	11
Italy	10	Scotland	72
Wales	21	France	20
France	24	England	18
Ireland	41	Scotland	8
Wales	95	Italy	0
England	12	Wales	15
Ireland	95	Italy	7
Scotland	8	France	16
Italy	13	England	79
France	51	Ireland	23
France	74	Italy	0
Ireland	25	Wales	17
Scotland	19	England	26
Wales	27	Scotland	25

	P	W	L	F	A	Pts
France	5	4	1	185	70	8
Wales	5	4	1	175	82	8
Ireland	5	3	2	195	103	6
England	5	3	2	155	82	6
Scotland	5	1	4	132	120	2
Italy	5	0	5	30	415	0

SANZAR U21 CHAMPIONSHIPS
(HELD IN AUCKLAND, NEW ZEALAND)

Final

New Zealand	71	South Africa	5

Third-place Play-off

Australia	44	England	24

Fifth-place Play-off

Argentina	38	Scotland	17

Seventh-place Play-off

Samoa	30	Tonga	15

WORLD JUNIOR CHAMPIONSHIP

Final

France	14	Australia	0

Third-place Play-off

New Zealand	36	Wales	8

18 GROUP AND SCHOOLS INTERNATIONALS 1999-2000

Scotland	3	France	32
Wales	22	Romania U19	7
Wales	8	France	25
Wales	34	Japan	30
Scotland	3	Scotland U18	8
England 'A'	20	Wales 'A'	21
England	31	Wales	15
Scotland	37	Spain U19	20
England	10	Ireland	13
Scotland	15	England Clubs	15
France	49	Ireland	24
France	13	England	10
Ireland	20	Wales	5

STUDENT AND UNIVERSITY INTERNATIONALS 1999-2000

English Univs	22	Welsh Univs	10
Scottish Univs	3	English Univs	57
Irish Colleges	29	English Univs	10
England Students	35	Irish Univs	14
French Univs	17	English Univs	9
England Students	20	Wales Students	25

THE TIMES INTERNATIONAL UNIVERSITIES TROPHY

Final

U of Pau (Bayonne) 19		U College Cork	8

HONG KONG SEVENS

Cup Final
New Zealand   31   Fiji   5

Plate Final
France   19   Croatia   14

Bowl Final
Ireland   59   China   7

IRB SEVENS SERIES FINALS

South Africa:
Fiji   12   New Zealand   10

Uruguay (Punto del Este):
New Zealand   42   Fiji   19

Argentina (Mar del Plata):
Fiji   26   New Zealand   14

New Zealand (Wellington):
Fiji   24   New Zealand   14

Fiji:
New Zealand   31   Fiji   5

Australia (Brisbane):
Fiji   24   Australia   21

Japan (Tokyo):
Fiji   27   New Zealand   22

OTHER INTERNATIONAL SEVENS FINALS

Dubai:
New Zealand   48   Fiji   14

Paris:
New Zealand   69   South Africa   10

TRI-NATIONS SERIES 2000

Results
Australia   35   New Zealand   39
New Zealand   25   South Africa   12
Australia   26   South Africa   6

At time of going to press

WOMEN'S FIVE NATIONS CHAMPIONSHIP 1999-2000

Results
England   31   Spain   7
Wales   10   France   24
France   18   England   24
Spain   13   Scotland   9
England   51   Wales   0
Scotland   7   France   10
France   38   Spain   5
Wales   12   Scotland   36
Scotland   9   England   64

Wales v Spain not played

	P	W	L	F	A	Pts
England	4	4	0	170	34	8
France	4	3	1	90	46	6
Scotland	4	1	3	61	99	2
Spain	3	1	2	25	78	2
Wales	3	0	3	22	111	0

FIRA WOMEN'S CHAMPIONSHIP

Semi-finals
England   12   France   19
Spain   13   Scotland   10

Third place play-off
England   40   Scotland   20

Final
France   31   Spain   0

CLUB, COUNTY AND DIVISIONAL RUGBY

ENGLAND

Tetley's Bitter Cup
Quarter-finals

Bristol	25	Harlequins	17
London Irish	34	Gloucester	18
London Welsh	26	Northampton	35
Wasps	62	Manchester	3

Semi-finals

Bristol	31	Wasps	44
London Irish	17	Northampton	24

Final

Wasps	31	Northampton	23

NPI Cup Final (Intermediate)

Dunstablians	14	Hull Ionians	10

Tetley's Bitter Vase Final (Junior)

Sheffield	20	Bank of England	11

Allied Dunbar Premiership
Premier One

	P	W	D	L	F	A	Pts
Leicester	22	18	1	3	687	425	51†
Bath	22	15	2	5	690	425	43†
Gloucester	22	15	0	7	628	490	40†
Saracens	22	14	0	8	729	514	37†
Northampton	22	13	0	9	551	480	35†
Bristol	22	12	1	9	632	602	34§
Wasps	22	11	1	10	640	461	31†
London Irish	22	9	1	12	613	616	25§
Newcastle	22	6	2	14	377	630	19§
Harlequins	22	7	0	15	441	687	18§
Sale	22	7	0	15	381	633	18§
Bedford	22	1	0	21	396	802	3

Relegated: Bedford

Premier Two

	P	W	D	L	F	A	Pts
Rotherham	26	24	0	2	1045	267	48§
Leeds Tykes	26	22	0	4	794	269	44
Worcester	26	19	0	7	865	450	38
Exeter	26	19	0	7	742	466	38
London Welsh	26	16	0	10	712	476	32
Coventry	26	15	0	11	714	589	30
Moseley	26	14	0	12	595	526	28
Manchester	26	11	0	15	513	671	22
Henley	26	10	1	15	599	696	21
Wakefield	26	10	0	16	547	638	20
Orrell	26	7	0	19	388	682	14
Waterloo	26	6	2	18	441	830	14
Rugby	26	6	1	19	408	905	13
W Hartlepool	26	1	0	25	216	1114	2

Promoted: Rotherham
Relegated: West Hartlepool

† Denotes qualified for European Cup
(Wasps as winners of Tetley's Bitter Cup)
§ Denotes qualified for European Shield

Jewson National League
1st Division Champions: Otley
Runners-up: Birmingham/Solihull
2nd Division North Champions: Kendal
Runners-up: Stourbridge
2nd Division South Champions: Esher
Runners-up: Penzance/Newlyn

Tetley's Bitter County Championship
Semi-finals

Cheshire	8	Devon	24
Yorkshire	46	Cornwall	15

Final

Yorkshire	16	Devon	9

Plate Final

Notts, Lincs, & Derbys	21	Kent	6

Tetley's Bitter U20 County Championship
Final

Yorkshire	43	East Midlands	38

University Match

Oxford U	16	Cambridge U	13

University Second Teams Match

OU Greyhounds	36	CU LX Club	18

University U21 Match

Oxford U	15	Cambridge U	13

Other U21 Match

CU Colleges	26	OU Whippets	17

Women's University Match

Oxford U	62	Cambridge U	0

British Universities Sports Association
Men's Final

U of N'thumbria	14	Loughborough U	8

Women's Final

Loughborough U	15	UWIC (Card Inst)	10

Hospitals Cup Winners: Imperial Medicals
Scottish Amicable Trophy

Barbarians	85	Leicester	10

Inter-Services Champions: The Army
London Sevens Winners: Oxford University
Shell-Rosslyn Park Schools Sevens
Festival Winners: Wellington College
Open Winners: Sedbergh
Colts Winners: Manchester GS
Junior Winners: Dwr-y-Felin
Preparatory School Winners: St Olave's
Girls Schools Winners: KES Stafford

Daily Mail Schools Day (at Twickenham)
U18 Cup Winners: Colston's Collegiate
U18 Vase Winners: Wallington CGS
U15 Cup Winners: Wellington College

Bread For Life Women's Cup Final

Richmond	13	Clifton	10

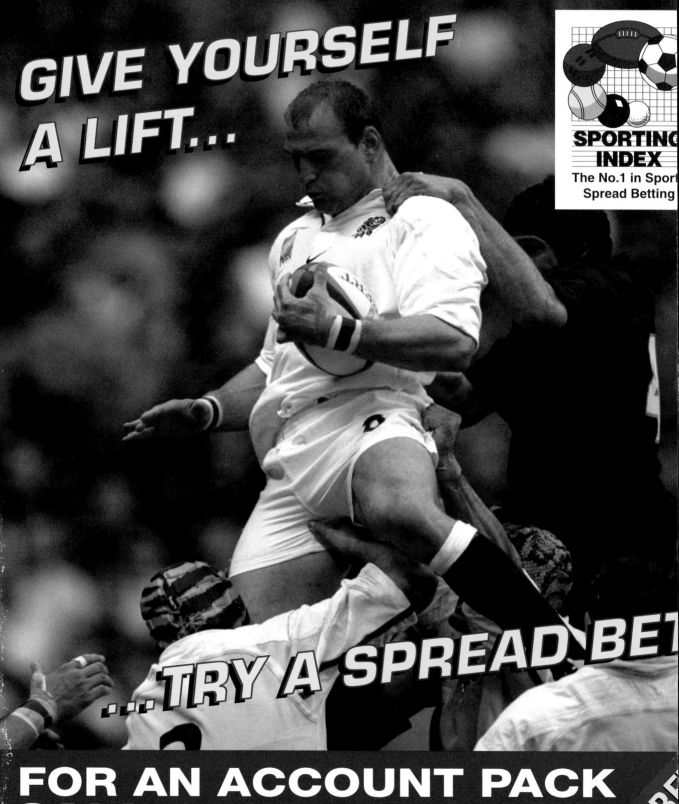

WALES

Challenge Cup
Semi-finals

Llanelli	38	Ebbw Vale	26
Swansea	32	Pontypridd	22

Final

Llanelli	22	Swansea	12

Welsh Scottish League

	P	W	D	L	F	A	Pts
Cardiff	22	18	1	3	879	504	59†
Newport	22	15	1	6	773	453	49†
Swansea	22	14	1	7	691	509	47†
Pontypridd	22	14	2	6	666	478	45†
Llanelli	22	13	0	9	748	527	38†
Ebbw Vale	22	12	0	10	647	569	38§
Neath	22	11	2	9	664	553	35§
Edinburgh Reivs	22	10	1	11	564	654	34†
Bridgend	22	8	1	13	427	564	27§
Glasgow Cals	22	8	1	13	488	621	25†
Caerphilly	22	2	1	19	427	939	6*§
Dunvant	22	1	1	20	357	960	5

Relegated: Dunvant
* Denotes points witheld

National Leagues
Division One

	P	W	D	L	F	A	Pts
Cross Keys	30	24	0	6	779	476	72§
Pontypool	30	22	1	7	845	450	67
Blackwood	30	21	1	8	688	507	64
Bonymaen	30	19	2	9	730	655	59
Tondu	30	16	2	12	650	568	50
Newbridge	30	14	2	14	783	742	44
Treorchy	30	14	1	15	611	565	43
Aberavon	30	13	0	17	776	666	39
Rumney	30	13	0	17	672	783	39
Abertillery	30	12	3	15	563	665	39
Llandovery	30	12	2	16	639	730	38
Llanharan	30	12	2	16	617	676	38
Abercynon	30	12	1	17	554	669	37
Merthyr	30	13	0	17	632	711	36*
Tredegar	30	12	0	18	588	710	30*
UWIC (Card Inst)	30	3	1	26	646	1104	10

Promoted: Cross Keys
Relegated: UWIC (Card Inst), Tredegar
* Denotes three points deducted
† Denotes qualified for European Cup
§ Denotes qualified for European Shield

2nd Division Champions: Glamorgan Wdrs
Runners-up: Carmarthen Quins
3rd Div East Champions: Brynmawr
Runners-up: Bedwas
3rd Div West Champions: Carmarthen Ath
Runners-up: Resolven

SCOTLAND

SRU Inter-District Championship

	P	W	L	F	A	Pts
Caledonia	3	3	0	123	79	6
Borders	3	2	1	112	83	4
Edinburgh	3	1	2	90	118	2
Glasgow	3	0	3	72	117	0

SRU BT Cellnet Cup Final
Boroughmuir   35   Glasgow Hawks 10

SRU BT Cellnet Shield Final
East Kilbride   27   G'gow Southern 17

SRU BT Cellnet Bowl Final
Murrayfield Wdrs   13   Linlithgow   5

Scottish Sevens Winners:
Kelso: Kelso
Selkirk: Jed-Forest
Gala: Melrose
Melrose: Nawaka (Fiji)
Peebles: Jed-Forest
Hawick: Hawick
Langholm: Hawick
Earlston: Gala
Jed-Forest: Kelso
Kings of Sevens: Melrose

SRU Tennents Velvet Premiership
Division One

	P	W	D	L	F	A	B	Pts
Heriot's FP	18	16	0	2	707	274	10	74
G'gow Hks	18	13	0	5	561	277	11	63
Melrose	18	11	0	7	446	396	8	52
Currie	18	10	0	8	436	442	12	52
Gala	18	9	0	9	457	448	10	46
Hawick	18	9	1	8	466	472	8	46
Jed-Forest	18	8	1	9	361	416	9	46
Watsonians	18	6	0	12	395	490	10	34
Kelso	18	5	0	13	323	531	7	27
W of Scot'd	18	2	0	16	276	687	5	13

Relegated: Kelso, West of Scotland

Division Two

	P	W	D	L	F	A	B	Pts
B'muir	18	15	2	1	723	213	13	77
Kirkcaldy	18	14	0	4	392	258	9	65
A'deen GSFP	18	12	1	5	478	294	11	61
Stirling C'ty	18	8	2	8	312	342	5	41
E Kilbride	18	8	1	9	283	343	6	40
Peebles	18	7	0	11	275	395	8	36
Selkirk	18	6	0	12	301	367	7	31
Biggar	18	5	3	10	232	359	7	31
M'lburgh	18	4	3	11	252	469	4	26
D'dee HSFP	18	5	0	13	334	542	3	23

Promoted: Boroughmuir, Kirkcaldy
Relegated: Dundee High School FP, Musselburgh

IRELAND

Inter-Provincial Championship

	P	W	L	F	A	B	Pts
Munster	6	6	0	242	103	4	28
Ulster	6	3	3	185	130	4	16
Leinster	6	3	3	146	136	1	13
Connacht	6	0	6	85	289	1	1

AIB All-Ireland League
Division One

	P	W	D	L	F	A	B	Pts
St Mary's C	11	8	0	3	265	121	4	36
Terenure C	11	8	0	3	235	229	4	36
Lansdowne	11	7	1	3	265	149	4	33
Ballymena	11	7	0	4	267	282	4	32
Garryowen	11	6	0	5	245	199	5	29
Cork Const	11	6	0	5	259	258	4	28
Y Munster	11	6	0	5	175	243	1	25
Buccaneers	11	5	0	6	205	196	2	22
Shannon	11	4	0	7	222	229	6	22
Dungannon	11	4	0	7	235	252	3	19
De la Salle-Palmerston	11	2	1	8	149	235	3	13
Clontarf	11	2	0	9	195	324	2	10

Champions: St Mary's College
Division One Play-off:

Clontarf	61	UC Dublin	56

(aggregate over two legs)

Division Two

	P	W	D	L	F	A	Pts
Blackrock Coll	14	12	1	1	465	178	50
Belfast H'quins	14	12	0	2	356	245	48
Old Crescent	14	11	1	2	317	196	46
Galwegians	14	11	0	3	360	202	44
Univ Coll Dublin	14	11	0	3	287	231	44
City of Derry	14	8	0	6	279	250	32
Old Belvedere	13	6	0	7	295	276	24
Sunday's Well	14	6	0	8	225	293	24
Dolphin	14	5	0	9	294	327	20
Univ College Cork	14	4	1	9	208	339	18
Bective Rangers	13	4	0	9	198	250	16
Malone	14	4	0	10	177	307	16
Greystones	14	3	1	10	290	442	14
Wanderers	14	3	0	11	271	349	12
Portadown	14	2	0	12	220	357	8

Champions: Blackrock College
Promoted: Belfast Harlequins, Old Crescent
Division Two Play-off:

Portadown	34	Instonians	34

(aggregate over two legs; Portadown retain senior status)

Promoted to Division Two: Bohemians, Midleton, Old Wesley, Ballynahinch, County Carlow

FRANCE

French Club Championship
Semi-finals

Stade Français	30	Toulouse	13
Colomiers	24	Pau	22

Final

Stade Français	28	Colomiers	23

French Cup Winners: Biarritz

ITALY

Italian League
Semi-finals

Roma	42	Viadana	19
L'Aquila	19	Treviso	17

Final

Roma	35	L'Aquila	17

NEW ZEALAND

Championship First Division 1999
Final

Auckland	24	Wellington	18

Ranfurly Shield Holders: Waikato

AUSTRALIA

Inter-State Final 1999

Queensland	24	NSW	3

BARBARIANS

Opponents	Results
Combined Services	W 45-26
Coventry	L 40-68
East Midlands	W 99-54
(Mobbs Memorial Match)	
Ireland	W 31-30
Scotland	W 45-42
Leicester	W 85-10
(Scottish Amicable Trophy)	

Played 6 Won 5 Lost 1

SUPER-12 TOURNAMENT 2000

Final Table

	P	W	D	L	F	A	B	Pts
Brumbies	11	9	0	2	393	196	9	45
Crusaders	11	8	0	3	369	293	7	39
Highlanders	11	6	0	5	323	280	8	32
Cats	11	7	0	4	320	334	4	32
Stormers	11	6	1	4	298	276	5	31
Blues	11	6	0	5	300	260	6	30
Reds	11	6	0	5	317	305	6	30
Hurricanes	11	6	0	5	308	329	5	29
Waratahs	11	5	0	6	276	258	5	25
Chiefs	11	3	0	8	257	352	8	20
Bulls	11	1	2	8	231	395	3	11
Sharks	11	1	1	9	233	341	3	9

Semi-finals

Brumbies 28 Cats 5 *(Canberra)*
Crusaders 37 Highlanders 15 *(Christchurch)*

Final

Brumbies 19 Crusaders 20 *(Canberra)*

Team names:
ACT Brumbies
Canterbury Crusaders
Otago Highlanders
Golden Cats
Western Stormers
Auckland Blues
Queensland Reds
Wellington Hurricanes
NSW Waratahs
Waikato Chiefs
Northern Bulls
Coastal Sharks

EUROPEAN CUP

Quarter-finals
Llanelli 22 Cardiff 3
Munster 27 Stade Français 10
Northampton 25 Wasps 22
Toulouse 31 Montferrand 18

Semi-finals
Northampton 31 Llanelli 28
Toulouse 25 Munster 31

Final
Northampton 9 Munster 8

EUROPEAN SHIELD

Quarter-finals
Biarritz 29 Bristol 32
Castres 43 Perpignan 33
Ebbw Vale 20 London Irish 21
Pau 36 Newcastle 20

Semi-finals
Castres 40 London Irish 30
Pau 51 Bristol 27

Final
Pau 34 Castres 21

PREVIEW OF THE SEASON 2000-01

KEY PLAYERS 2000-01

BY IAN ROBERTSON

ENGLAND

PHIL GREENING

England have shown a great deal of consistency in their forward selection during the reign of Clive Woodward. The back row of Hill, Dallaglio and Back has been an automatic selection, just as Johnson and Grewcock have been the first-choice locks. The choice at hooker has been more variable, with Mark Regan giving way to Richard Cockerill before Phil Greening took over and became the first choice right through the World Cup and the whole of last season.

By the summer of 2000 Greening had played 20 Tests for England and he is now a key player because he fits perfectly into Clive Woodward's view of the modern hooker. He throws in to the line out well and is a good scrummager, but most important of all he is a dynamic player in the open. He has the speed and ball skills of a back-row forward and has a great knack of turning up in the threequarter line in loose play with devastating effect. He also does his fair share of tackling and his all-round ability means he is likely to be an important figure not just for England but for the British Lions on their tour of Australia.

MIKE TINDALL

At the start of last season, the first-choice centre pairing at Bath would have been Jeremy Guscott and Mike Catt. By the end of the World Cup in November, Guscott had retired from international rugby and a new name exploded on to the scene. Not only did Mike Tindall establish himself quickly in the Bath side, he soon made himself an automatic selection for England.

A strong, forthright runner, Tindall ideally complemented Mike Catt, with his silky skills, at both club and national level, and it must have been very encouraging for the England manager, Clive Woodward, to see how well the back division

developed as an attacking force after the inclusion of Tindall. Tindall settled into his new role with England very quickly, scoring a try in his first international, which was against Ireland at Twickenham. He played in all the Six Nations matches and in both Tests against South Africa in the summer. A good tackler, he brings different talents to the England midfield from Guscott. Still only 21 at the start of this season, he looks sure to be a long-term and important figure in the England set-up.

FRANCE

CHRISTOPHE LAMAISON

The French have flattered to deceive for much of the past ten years and it was arguably only in the semi-finals of the World Cup, when they played magnificently to comprehensively defeat New Zealand, that they showed their full potential. On that occasion at Twickenham they were irresistible and contributed to one of the best and most memorable matches of the decade.

A major element in their improved form has been the play of Lamaison at fly half. The French have lacked a player of authority and experience in that key position for some time and indeed a great deal of their failure to hit the heights in recent years has been their inability to find a pair of outstanding half backs. Lamaison has changed all that. He has excellent hands and is a good kicker. He calls the shots in the French back division and has at long last given shape and balance to the team. Without him in the Six Nations they looked rudderless and all at sea. With him this season they could be difficult to beat.

FABIEN PELOUS

Part of the French forward problem in recent years has been their lack of discipline in tight games, which has resulted in them giving away a lot of penalties and suffering all sorts of crises of confidence as a result. All that seems to have changed with the emergence last season of Fabien Pelous, not just as a great lock forward but also as a strong and highly respected leader.

The French need a good captain, and Pelous seems ideal for that role. He is a top-class player who is outstanding at the line out and he is also tremendous for such a big man in the open. He popped up all over the field in France's great World Cup run and was just as effective when charging down the pitch with the ball in his hands as he was when putting in thundering tackles. Pelous has the

wealth of experience that comes from playing 53 Tests for his country and he has learned from the mistakes of the past. Along with coach Bernard Laporte he can help France fulfil their full potential.

IRELAND

BRIAN O'DRISCOLL

The Irish have a happy knack of producing, every few years, a really outstanding midfield player who becomes an institution in the team and around whom they can build their tactics. Brian O'Driscoll looks destined to be their star centre over the foreseeable future and he is likely to be a key player for the British Lions tour to Australia in the summer of 2001. He has all the attributes of a top-class centre in the new, modern, professional game. Defence is very important nowadays and he is a strong, aggressive, determined tackler. In attack he has the perfect blend of power and speed and an eye for the gap. He has good acceleration and he is an elusive runner with excellent hands – he is one of the most incisive and exciting backs in world rugby.

O'Driscoll is going to be the linchpin of the Irish back division and he could be even more devastatingly effective when he is surrounded by a host of great players on the Lions tour. His problem with Ireland is that the opposition will concentrate on stopping him at all costs this season after his success in the last campaign, but he will be good enough to take that sort of pressure.

PETER STRINGER

Ireland have not had an established half-back pairing of top quality during the past few years and that has adversely affected their back play. Last season things started to look up with the arrival of Ronan O'Gara and Peter Stringer, who teamed up with the added considerable influence of another newcomer, Brian O'Driscoll in the centre. It has to be said at this early stage of their careers that O'Gara and Stringer have great potential, but they still have to develop into top-class players. Stringer won his first cap last season at the age of 22 and he settled in very quickly to fulfil all the basic duties of a scrum half. He has a fast, accurate pass and he is capable of making a decent break, although he needs to work on this.

It is important for a scrum half to avoid being predictable by passing the ball every time to his fly half and Stringer needs to bring more variety to his play. The fact is he can break, he can kick and he can link and work with his loose forwards, so what he needs now is to gain experience of playing at the highest level. An extended run this season could see him establish himself in the Irish team alongside O'Gara.

ITALY

MAURO BERGAMASCO

For several seasons Diego Dominguez and Massimo Giovanelli have been the stars of the Italian team and without doubt they have been players of the highest class. There is every possibility that the next Italian superstar will be Mauro Bergamasco. He exploded on to the scene last year as a 20-year-old of considerable potential, and by the end of the Six Nations Championship he was not just the best forward in the Italian team he had also emerged as one of the best forwards in the northern hemisphere.

Under the coaching of former All Black prop forward Brad Johnstone, Bergamasco should be in the best possible finishing school and he has unquestionably got all the raw talent to be a great flank forward. He is a natural footballer and he is an excellent support player. He is quick round the pitch and seems to have a great instinct for being in the right place at the right time in the open. Bergamasco is also a strong defensive player and seems to relish the physical challenge. He won his first cap when he was only 19 and he should be the most influential forward in the Italian side for many years to come.

LUCA MARTIN

It was always going to be a very difficult year for Italy when they entered the Six Nations Championship for the first time and they emerged with credit at the end of the day with a well-deserved win over Scotland and some bold and brave performances in defeat in the other matches. They were held together all the way through by their brilliant fly half, Diego Dominguez, but his intention to retire has made it important for them to find another outstanding player to spearhead their attack.

Luca Martin is the player to take that role. By the start of this season he had already won 23 caps and he has scored nine tries in international rugby. He has scored most of those tries against England, Scotland, Wales and France, which proves he is a real force at the highest level. He is a strong, forthright runner who reads the game well, and he can bring the best out of those around him, just as Dominiguez did in recent years. Life will be very tough for Italy, but Martin can be their inspiration.

SCOTLAND

CHRIS PATERSON

When people north of the border start to think of Andy Irvine and Gavin Hastings at the mention of Chris Paterson, Scotland's new full back, we know the Scots have unearthed a player of dramatically above average ability. The very fact that Paterson was able to force his way into the international side at the expense of Glenn Metcalfe was proof he was a very accomplished player indeed. Metcalfe, an outstanding player himself, has switched to the wing to accommodate the multi-talented Paterson.

Paterson won his first cap in 2000 at the age of 21 and he rapidly showed he had the skill and the confidence to play Test rugby. He has good acceleration and sustained speed and he is also an elusive runner in attack. A safe pair of hands at full back under the high ball, he is at his best when he counter attacks from his own half. He is also excellent at joining the line as a running full back to create the overlap from set-piece play and from second-phase possession, and he is now a major attacking force in the Scotland side. He is a sound, solid defensive player with an exciting future ahead of him.

BUDGE POUNTNEY

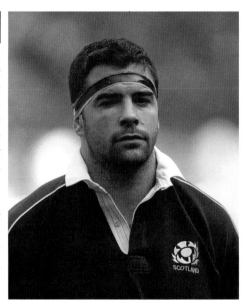

The list of outstanding Scottish back-row forwards is long, and the Scots also often produce a great blend of loose forwards. Finlay Calder, Derek White and John Jeffrey ruled the roost in their heyday and this season Scotland are likely to have two of the best flankers in the northern hemisphere in Budge Pountney and Martin Leslie. Pountney was in great form for both his club side, Northampton, and also for his country. He won his first cap at the age of 26, but he very quickly established himself as a top-class forward and he is now arguably the most important forward in the Scottish team.

Pountney is a tremendously strong, aggressive defensive player who shores up his side of the scrum with fierce determination. He is also a very abrasive, physical attacking player with the ball in his hands. He has the requisite speed and strength and is not only good at launching the initial attack and working in concert with the other loose forwards and the half backs, he is also fully capable of inspiring the Scottish forwards to hit the heights consistently this season.

WALES

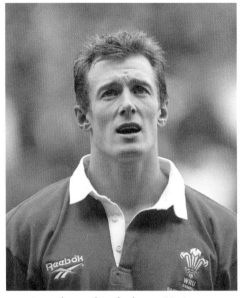

ROB HOWLEY

When you consider how a couple of years ago Rob Howley was unquestionably the best scrum half in the northern hemisphere it is very hard to think he is suddenly no longer capable of guiding Wales to glory. In the space of a few months he lost the captaincy of the Welsh team and then to general surprise outside the Principality he lost his place in the Welsh side. The fact is he may have lost his very best form for one reason or another last season but he has definitely not become a bad player overnight.

He has been generally regarded as the most complete all-round scrum half in Europe for four years. Those skills do not disappear. He still has the fastest, most accurate pass when he is on top of his game and he has a lethal ability to break from both set-piece play and in the loose. He is a great tactical kicker and works well with his loose forwards. Above all he is an inspirational figure with a wealth of experience, and the fact is if Wales are to have a really good year they desperately need the genius of Rob Howley.

CHRIS WYATT

The Welsh have produced some good results since Graham Henry took over the coaching, but it is probably true to say they have not had players in their pack who have stood supreme in the eye of their opponents the way Martin Johnson and Lawrence Dallaglio have for England. It seems the need for a commanding figure up front is a matter of importance and the name of Chris Wyatt is high on the list of people who could fulfil that role. He came into the Welsh side in the summer of 1998 and went on to win 21 caps over the next two years before apparently losing his form and being dropped.

It is always interesting how the prospect of a British Lions tour helps to concentrate the mind and that may be just the focus Wyatt needs to get back to his very best and make a major contribution to the Welsh effort. He is a good, solid scrummager and certainly capable of winning his full share of line-out ball. He is mobile in the open and fits the bill as a lock forward made for the new, professional game. If he hits top form he could be a most influential player.

FIXTURES 2000-01

Note: No venue given for a representative match indicates that the ground was yet to be announced at the time of going to press.

AUGUST 2000

Sat, 5th — Ulster v Leicester (Charity Match, Omagh)

Sat, 12th — Middlesex Sevens (Twickenham)
Cardiff v Leicester (Challenge Shield, Cardiff)

Sat, 19th — Zurich Prem Lge (1)

Sat, 26th — Zurich Prem Lge (2)
Welsh Scottish League (1)
Welsh League Divs 1/2(1)

SEPTEMBER 2000

Sat, 2nd — Zurich Prem Lge (3)
English National Lgs 2/3N/3S (1)
National Lgs (12s) (1) England
Scottish Prem (1); Nat Lgs (2)
Welsh Challenge Cup (1st Round)
Welsh Scottish League (2)
Welsh Leagues Divs 1/2 (2)
Welsh Leagues Divs 3E/3W (1)

Tue, 5th &
Wed, 6th — Zurich Prem Lge (4)
Welsh Scottish League (3)

Sat, 9th — Zurich Prem Lge (5)
English National Lge 1 (1); 2 (2)
Tetley's Bitter Cup (Prelim Rd)
NPI Cup (1st Round)
Tetley's Bitter Vase (1st Round)
Scottish Prem (2); Nat Lgs (2)
Scottish Cups (1st Round)
Welsh Scottish League (4)
Welsh Leagues Divs 1/2 (3)
Welsh Leagues Divs 3E/3W (2)
Welsh Leagues Divs 4E/4W (1)

Sat, 16th — Zurich Prem Lge (6)
English National Lge 1 (2); 2 (3)
English National Lgs 3N/3S (2)
National Lgs (12s) (2) England
National Lgs (10s) (1) England
Scottish Prem (3); Nat Lgs (3)
Welsh Scottish League (5)
Welsh Leagues Divs 1/2 (4)
Welsh Leagues Divs 3E/3W (3)
Welsh Leagues Divs 4E/4W (2)

Sat, 23rd — Tetley's Bitter Cup (1st Round)
Zurich Prem Lge (7)
English National Lge 1 (3); 2 (4)
English National Lgs 3N/3S (3)
National Lgs (12s) (3) England
National Lgs (10s) (2) England

Scottish Prem (4); Nat Lgs (4)
Welsh Challenge Cup (2nd Round)
Welsh Scottish League (6)
Welsh Leagues Divs 1/2 (5)
Welsh Leagues Divs 3E/3W (4)

Sat, 30th — Zurich Prem Lge (8)
English National Lge 1 (4); 2 (5)
English National Lgs 3N/3S (4)
National Lgs (12s) (4) England
National Lgs (10s) (3) England
Scottish Prem (5); Nat Lgs (5)
Welsh Scottish League (7)
Welsh Leagues Divs 1/2 (6)
Welsh Leagues Divs 3E/3W (5)
Welsh Leagues Divs 4E/4W (3)

OCTOBER 2000

Fri, 6th –
Sun, 8th — Heineken Cup (1)

Sat, 7th — English National Lge 1 (5); 2 (6)
Tetley's Bitter Cup (2nd Round)
NPI Cup (2nd Round)
Tetley's Bitter Vase (2nd Round)
Scottish Prem (6); Nat Lgs (6)
Welsh Leagues Divs 1/2 (7)
Welsh Leagues Divs 3E/3W (6)
Welsh Leagues Divs 4E/4W (4)

Fri, 13th –
Sun, 15th — Heineken Cup (2)

Sat, 14th — English National Lge 1 (6); 2 (7)
English National Lgs 3N/3S (5)
National Lgs (12s) (5) England
National Lgs (10s) (4) England
Scottish Premier Lgs (7)
Scottish Cups (2nd Round)
AIB (IRFU) Division 2 (1)
Welsh Challenge Cup (3rd Round)
Welsh Leagues Divs 1/2 (8)

Fri, 20th –
Sun, 22nd — Heineken Cup (3)

Sat, 21st — Tetley's Bitter Cup (3rd Round)
English National Lge 1 (7); 2 (8)
English National Lgs 3N/3S (6)
National Lgs (12s) (6) England
National Lgs (10s) (5) England
Scottish Prem (8); Nat Lgs (7)
Welsh Leagues Divs 1/2 (9)
Welsh Leagues Divs 3E/3W (7)
Welsh Leagues Divs 4E/4W (5)
AIB (IRFU) Division 2 (2)

Fri, 27th –
Sun, 29th — Heineken Cup (4)

Sat, 28th — English National Lge 1 (8); 2 (9)
English National Lgs 3N/2S (7)

National Lgs (12s) (7) England
Scottish Prem (9); Nat Lgs (8)
Welsh Leagues Divs 1/2 (10)
Welsh Leagues Divs 3E/3W (8)
Welsh Leagues Divs 4E/4W (6)

NOVEMBER 2000

Sat, 4th   FRANCE v AUSTRALIA
SCOTLAND v USA (Perth)
English National Lge 1 (9)
Tetley's Bitter Cup (4th Round)
NPI Cup (3rd Round)
Tetley's Bitter Vase (3rd Round)
Welsh Scottish League (8)
Welsh Leagues Div 1 (11)
Scottish Cups (3rd Round)

Tue, 7th   Combined Services v Barbarians
(Aldershot)

Sat, 11th   FRANCE v NEW ZEALAND
IRELAND v JAPAN (Dublin)
SCOTLAND v AUSTRALIA
(Murrayfield)
WALES v SAMOA (Cardiff)
Tetley's Bitter Cup (5th Round)
English National Lge 1 (10); 2 (10)
English National Lgs 3N/3S (8)
National Lgs (12s) (8) England
National Lgs (10s) (6) England
Welsh Leagues Div 1 (12); 2 (11)

Sat, 11th or
Sun, 12   Welsh Scottish League (9)

Sat, 18th   ENGLAND v AUSTRALIA
(Twickenham)
ITALY v CANADA
SCOTLAND v SAMOA
(Murrayfield)
WALES v USA (Cardiff)
Zurich Prem Lge (9)
English National Lge 1 (11); 2 (11)
English National Lgs 3N/3S (9)
National Lgs (12s) (9) England
Welsh Leagues Div 1 (13); 2 (12)

Sat 18th or
Sun, 19th   Welsh Leagues Divs 3E/3W (9)
or 24th Feb Welsh Leagues Divs 4E/4W (7)

Sun, 19th   IRELAND v SOUTH AFRICA
(Dublin)
Scottish National Lgs (9)

Sat, 25th   ENGLAND v ARGENTINA
(Twickenham)
ITALY v NEW ZEALAND
WALES v SOUTH AFRICA
(Cardiff)
Zurich Prem Lge (10)
English National Lgs 1/2 (12)
English National Lgs 3N/3S (10)
Scottish Prem (10); Nat Lgs (10)
Welsh Scottish League (10)
Welsh Leagues Div 1 (14); 2 (13)

Welsh Leagues Divs 3E/3W (10)
Welsh Leagues Divs 4E/4W (8)

Tue, 29th   Combined Services v South Africa
(Aldershot)

DECEMBER 2000

Sat, 2nd   ENGLAND v SOUTH AFRICA
(Twickenham)
Zurich Prem Lge (11)
English National Lge 2 (13)
English National Lgs 3N/3S (11)
Tetley's Bitter Cup (Qtr-finals)
NPI Cup (4th Round)
Tetley's Bitter Vase (4th Round)
Scottish Cups (4th Round)
Welsh Scottish League (11)
Welsh Leagues Div 1 (15); 2 (14)
Welsh Leagues Divs 3E/3W (11)
Welsh Leagues Divs 4E/4W (9)
AIB (IRFU) Division 1 (1); 2 (3)

Sat, 9th   English National Lge 1 (13)
English National Lgs 3N/3S (12)
National Lgs (12s) (11) England
National Lgs (10s) (8) England
Scottish Prem (11); Nat Lgs (12)
Welsh Scottish League (13)
Welsh Challenge Cup (4th Round)
Welsh Leagues Divs 3E/3W (12)
AIB (IRFU) Division 1 (2); 2 (4)

Tue, 12th   Oxford v Cambridge
(Bowring Bowl, Twickenham)
Oxford U21 v Cambridge U21
(Bowring Plate, Twickenham)

Sat, 16th   Zurich Prem Lge (12)
English National Lgs 1/2 (14)
English National Lgs 3N/3S (13)
National Lgs (12s) (12) England
National Lgs (10s) (9) England
Scottish Cups (5th Round)
Welsh Scottish League (14)
Welsh Leagues Div 1 (16); 2 (15)
Welsh Leagues Divs 3E/3W (12)
Welsh Leagues Divs 4E/4W (10)
AIB (IRFU) Division 1 (3); 2 (5)

Sat, 23rd   Zurich Prem Lge (13)
English National Lge 2 (15)
English National Lgs 3N/3S (14)
Welsh Leagues Div 1 (17); 2 (16)
Welsh Leagues Divs 3E/3W (13)
Welsh Leagues Divs 4E/4W (11)
AIB (IRFU) Division 1 (4)
Bohemians v Ballynahinch (AIB 2)

Tue, 26th or
Wed, 27th   Welsh Scottish League (16)
Wed, 27th   Zurich Prem Lge (14)
Sat, 30th   Zurich Prem Lge (15)
English National Lge 1 (15)
English National Lgs 3N/3S (15)
Scottish Premier Lgs (12)
Welsh Leagues Div 2 (17)

Welsh Leagues Divs 3E/3W (14)
Welsh Leagues Divs 4E/4W (12)
AIB (IRFU) Division 1 (5); 2 (6)

JANUARY 2001

Sat, 6th
Tetley's Bitter Cup (Semi-finals)
Zurich Prem Lge (16)
English National Lgs 2/3N/3S (16)
NPI Cup (5th Round)
Tetley's Bitter Vase (5th Round)
National Lgs (12s) (13) England
Scottish National Lgs (12)
Welsh Leagues Divs 1/2 (18)
Welsh Leagues Divs 3E/3W (15)
Welsh Leagues Divs 4E/4W (13)
AIB (IRFU) Division 1 (6); 2 (7)

Fri, 12th –
Sun, 14th   Heineken Cup (5)
Sat, 13th   English National Lge 1 (16)
English National Lgs 2/3N/3S (17)
National Lgs (12s) (14) England
National Lgs (10s) (10) England
Scottish Prem (13); Nat Lgs (13)
AIB (IRFU) Division 2 (8)
Welsh Leagues Divs 1/2 (19)
Welsh Leagues Divs 3E/3W (16)
Welsh Leagues Divs 4E/4W (14)

Fri, 19th –
Sun, 21st   Heineken Cup (6)
Sat, 20th   English National Lge 1 (17)
English National Lgs 2/3N/3S (18)
National Lgs (12s) (15) England
National Lgs (10s) (11) England
Welsh Challenge Cup (5th Rd, prov)
Welsh Leagues Divs 1/2 (20)
Welsh Leagues Divs 3E/3W (17)
Welsh Leagues Divs 4E/4W (15)
AIB (IRFU) Division 2 (9)
Scottish Cups (Quarter-finals)

Fri, 26th –
Sun, 28th   Heineken Cup (Quarter-finals)
Sat, 27th   NPI Cup (6th Round)
Tetley's Bitter Vase (6th Round)
English National Lgs 2/3N/3S (19)
National Lgs (12s) (16) England
National Lgs (10s) (12) England
Welsh Leagues Divs 1/2 (21)
Welsh Leagues Divs 3E/3W (18)
Welsh Leagues Divs 4E/4W (16)
Scottish Prem (14); Nat Lgs (14)
Bohemians v City of Derry (AIB 2)

FEBRUARY 2001

Fri, 2nd
Italy 'A' v Ireland 'A'
Italy U21 v Ireland U21
Wales 'A' v England 'A'
Wales U21 v England U21
Sat, 3rd   ITALY v IRELAND (Rome, 2pm)
WALES v ENGLAND (Cardiff, 4pm)

France 'A' v Scotland 'A'
France U21 v Scotland U21
English National Lge 2 (18)
Sun, 4th   FRANCE v SCOTLAND (Paris, tba)
Sat, 10th   Zurich Prem Lge (17)
English National Lge 1 (19)
English National Lgs 2/3N/3S (20)
National Lgs (12s) (17) England
National Lgs (10s) (13) England
Scottish Prem (15); Nat Lgs (15)
Welsh Scottish League (17)
Welsh Leagues Divs 1/2 (22)
Welsh Leagues Divs 3E/3W (19)
Welsh Leagues Divs 4E/4W (17)
AIB (IRFU) Division 1 (7); 2 (10)

Fri, 16th   England 'A' v Italy 'A'
England U21 v Italy U21
Ireland 'A' v France 'A'
Ireland U21 v France U21
Scotland 'A' v Wales 'A'
Scotland U21 v Wales U21
Sat, 17th   IRELAND v FRANCE (Dublin, 2pm)
ENGLAND v ITALY
        (Twickenham, 2.30)
SCOTLAND v WALES
        (Murrayfield, 4pm)
Sat, 24th   Tetley's Bitter Cup Final
        (Twickenham)
English National Lge 1 (20)
English National Lgs 2/3N/3S (21)
NPI Cup (Quarter-finals)
Tetley's Bitter Vase (Qtr-finals)
National Lgs (12s) (18) England
National Lgs (10s) (14) England
Scottish Prem (16); Nat Lgs (16)
Welsh Challenge Cup (6th Rd, prov)
Welsh Leagues Divs 1/2 (23)
Welsh Leagues Divs 3E/3W (20)
AIB (IRFU) Division 1 (8); 2 (11)

MARCH 2001

Fri, 2nd
England 'A' v Scotland 'A'
England U21 v Scotland U21
Italy 'A' v France 'A'
Italy U21 v France U21
Wales 'A' v Ireland 'A'
Wales U21 v Ireland U21
Sat, 3rd   ITALY v FRANCE (Rome, 2pm)
ENGLAND v SCOTLAND
        (Twickenham, 2.30pm)
WALES v IRELAND (Cardiff, 4pm)
Sat, 10th   Zurich Prem Lge (19)
English National Lge 1 (21)
English National Lgs 2/3N/3S (22)
National Lgs (12s) (19) England
National Lgs (10s) (15) England
Scottish Prem (17); Nat Lgs (17)
Welsh Scottish League (18)
Welsh Leagues Divs 1/2 (24)

	Welsh Leagues Divs 3E/3W (21)
	Welsh Leagues Divs 4E/4W (18)
	AIB (IRFU) Division 1 (9); 2 (12)
Fri, 16th	France 'A' v Wales 'A'
	France U21 v Wales U21
	Scotland 'A' v Italy 'A'
	Scotland U21 v Italy U21
Sat, 17th	FRANCE v WALES (Paris, 2pm)
	SCOTLAND v ITALY
	(Murrayfield, 4pm)
	NPI Cup (Semi-finals)
	Tetley's Bitter Vase (Semi-finals)
	Zurich Prem Lge (20)
	English National Lge 1 (22)
	English National Lgs 2/3N/3S (23)
	National Lgs (12s) (20) England
	National Lgs (10s) (16) England
	AIB (IRFU) Division 1 (10)
Wed, 21st	BUSA Championships finals
	(Twickenham)
Fri, 23rd	Ireland 'A' v England 'A'
	Ireland U21 v England U21
Sat, 24th	IRELAND v ENGLAND (Dublin, 3pm)
	English National Lge 1 (23)
	English National Lgs 2/3N/3S (24)
	Scottish Prem (18); Nat Lgs (18)
	Welsh Chall Cup (Qtr-finals, prov)
	Welsh Leagues Divs 1/2 (25)
	Welsh Leagues Divs 3E/3W (22)
	Welsh Leagues Divs 4E/4W (19)
Wed, 28th	RAF v Royal Navy (Gloucester)
Sat, 31st	Zurich Prem Lge (21)
	English National Lge 1 (24)
	English National Lgs 2/3N/3S (25)
	National Lgs (12s) (21) England
	National Lgs (10s) (17) England
	Welsh Scottish League (19)
	Welsh Leagues Divs 1/2 (26)
	Welsh Leagues Divs 3E/3W (23)
	Welsh Leagues Divs 4E/4W (20)
	AIB (IRFU) Division 1 (11); 2 (13)
	Scottish Cups (Semi-finals)

APRIL 2001

Wed, 4th	The Army v RAF (Aldershot)
Fri, 6th	England 'A' v France 'A'
	England U21 v France U21
	Scotland 'A' v Ireland 'A'
	Scotland U21 v Ireland U21
Sat, 7th	ENGLAND v FRANCE
	(Twickenham, 2.30pm)
	SCOTLAND v IRELAND
	(Murrayfield, 1.45pm)
	Italy 'A' v Wales 'A'
	Italy U21 v Wales U21
Sun, 8th	ITALY v WALES (Rome, 2pm)
Sat, 14th	Zurich Prem Lge (22)
	English National Lge 1 (25)
	English National Lgs 2/3N/3S (26)

	National Lgs (12s) (22) England
	National Lgs (10s) (18) England
	Welsh Challenge Cup
	(Semi-finals, prov)
	Welsh Leagues Divs 1/2 (27)
	Welsh Leagues Divs 3E/3W (24)
	Welsh Leagues Divs 4E/4W (21)
	AIB (IRFU) Division 1 (12); 2 (14)
Fri, 20th–	
Sun, 22nd	Heineken Cup (Semi-finals)
Sat, 21st	NPI Cup Final (Twickenham)
	Tetley's Bitter Vase Final
	(Twickenham)
	Welsh Scottish League (20)
	Welsh Leagues Divs 1/2 (28)
	Welsh Leagues Divs 3E/3W (25)
	Welsh Leagues Divs 4E/4W (22)
	AIB (IRFU) Division 1 (13); 2 (15)
Sat, 28th	Zurich Premier Lge Play-off
	(Quarter-finals)
	English National Lge 1 (26)
	Scottish Cups Finals Day
	(Murrayfield)
	Welsh Scottish League (21)
	Welsh Leagues Divs 1/2 (29)
	Welsh Leagues Divs 3E/3W (26)

MAY 2001

Sat, 5th	Zurich Premier Lge Play-off
	(Semi-finals)
	County Championship (Qtr-finals)
	Welsh Scottish League (22)
	Welsh Leagues Divs 1/2 (30)
	AIB (IRFU) Division 1 (14)
	Royal Navy v The Army
	(Twickenham)
Sun, 6th	Garryowen v Y Munster (AIB 1)
Sat, 12th	Zurich Prem Lge Grand Final
	(Twickenham)
	County Championship
	(Semi-finals)
Sat, 19th or	
Sun, 20th	Heineken Cup Final
	Welsh Challenge Cup Final
	(provisional)
	Nat Lge Play-offs (12s,10s)
	(England)
	AIB (IRFU) Division 1 (15)
Sat, 26th	County Championship Finals
	(Twickenham)
Sun, 27th	Scottish Amicable Trophy
	(Twickenham)

Mission Statement

The Wooden Spoon Society aims to enhance the quality
and prospect of life for children and young persons in the
United Kingdom who are presently disadvantaged either
physically, mentally or socially

Charity Registration No: 326691